ROSES AND RADICALS

THE EPIC STORY OF HOW AMERICAN WOMEN WON THE RIGHT TO VOTE

ROSES AND RADICALS

THE EPIC STORY OF HOW AMERICAN WOMEN WON THE RIGHT TO VOTE

BY
SUSAN ZIMET
&
TODD HASAK-LOWY

Mr. PRESIDENT
HOW LONG
MUST
WOMEN WAIT
FOR LIBERTY

PUFFIN BOOKS

PUFFIN BOOKS

An imprint of Penguin Random House LLC, New York

First published in the United States of America by Viking, an imprint of Penguin Random House LLC, 2018
Published by Puffin Books, an imprint of Penguin Random House LLC, 2020

Copyright © 2018 by Susan Zimet

Visit us online at penguinrandomhouse.com

LIBRARY OF CONGRESS CATALOGING-IN-PUBLICATION DATA IS AVAILABLE.
ISBN 9780425291467

Printed in U.S.A.   Set in Kepler Light   Book design by Nancy Brennan

1   3   5   7   9   10   8   6   4   2

PHOTO CREDITS

pp. ii-iii, 8, 15, 20, 24, 40, 45, 48, 50, 55, 61, 65, 87, 89, 96, 99, 104, 120, 126, 144, 146, 155: Library of Congress Prints and Photographs Division / p. 12: New York Public Library, Art and Picture Collection / p. 17: National Portrait Gallery, Smithsonian Institution; gift of Mrs. Alan Valentine / p. 34: Chester County Historical Society, West Chester, PA / p. 60: National Portrait Gallery, Smithsonian Institution / p. 82: Photograph by Matthew Brady, Harvard Art Museum/Fogg Museum, Historical Photographs and Special Visual Collections Department, Fine Arts Library / p. 107: Photograph by Mary Garrity, National Portrait Gallery, Smithsonian Institution / p. 110: Art by Henry "Hy" Mayer; restored by Adam Cuerden, Cornell University – PJ Mode Collection of Persuasive Cartography / pp. 118, 123, 137: Library of Congress Manuscript Division, Records of the National Woman's Party / p. 140: Courtesy of the Lester S. Levy Collection of Sheet Music, The Sheridan Libraries, The Johns Hopkins University

To today's suffragists,
Hannah Auerbach, Sara Weiss,
and Ariel and Noam Hasak-Lowy.
May your dreams come true as you conquer the world.

And to our new addition to the suffragist collective, Lily Auerbach.
May the ERA be passed and all your rights protected
as you conquer the world.

CONTENTS

Foreword ✧ 1

Introduction ✧ 4

CHAPTER 1:
Enough of the Everlasting No ✧ 7

CHAPTER 2:
A Leader Emerges and a Resolution
Is Made ✧ 21

CHAPTER 3:
The Great Partnership ✧ 42

CHAPTER 4:
Postwar Turbulence ✧ 57

CHAPTER 5:

A Vote, a Trial, and the Long, Long Road
to Suffrage ✷ 73

CHAPTER 6:

British Tactics and New Leadership
on Parade ✷ 93

CHAPTER 7:

The Long Showdown and a Night
of Terror ✷ 111

CHAPTER 8:

War of the Roses: The Final Battle
for the Right to Vote ✷ 129

Epilogue ✷ 147

Source Notes ✷ 151

Bibliography ✷ 155

Acknowledgments ✷ 157

Index ✷ 158

Foreword

WARNING: THE BOOK YOU HOLD IN YOUR HAND MAY HAVE the power to change your life.

I hated that my history books were populated with the stories of white men, when I was a student. I wanted a history of people like me, ordinary women who changed the world. I wanted bottom-up history, not top-down history.

History is not what happened; it's the story someone tells us about what happened, from their perspective. What biases do they have? How much information? History is not static. It's not an end; it's a process. It's not a noun; it's a verb. History changes when the outsiders come in armed with their perspective and information.

In the 1960s when people of color, LGBTQ folks, and women, among others, began organizing for our rightful place in society, we invaded the history books, demanding that our stories be told. How did women gain a political voice? The old history told us male leaders gave it to us. Wrong. A movement of women, assisted by their male allies, demanded and won it.

When the National Woman Suffrage Association leaders Elizabeth Cady Stanton, Matilda Joslyn Gage, and Susan B. Anthony set out to document their movement's history, there was no internet. They relied on their own papers and memories, telling the story through their lens. After Gage and Stanton died, Anthony worked with her handpicked biographer, Ida Husted Harper, to edit two more volumes of the history. Harper added a sixth volume after Anthony's death. While Stanton and Gage had championed causes from pay equity to reproductive justice, Anthony focused exclusively on the vote. As Anthony's perspective held sway, the broader story became condensed to the paltry information in history textbooks telling students that Anthony and Stanton alone led a seventy-two-year undeviating struggle to win the right to vote.

That's where *Roses and Radicals* begins. But quickly it expands the lens. With Stanton and Anthony as the backdrop, it repopulates history with important women usually left out of textbook summaries, like Gage, who dropped out in protest as the movement became more conservative. It enriches the story, frankly acknowledging the internal struggles and political differences among the women. Stanton's racism, along with that of the movement after the radical National Woman Suffrage Association merged with the more conservative American Woman Suffrage Association, is faced squarely with no hedging, as are the differences between the two organizations in focus and strategy.

I wish I'd had this book when I was a student. It could have changed my life. I would have understood that we all can make a difference in the world. We're not born into activism; something triggers it. Stanton got jump-started by watching women delegates excluded from a convention, and Anthony initially acted from anger at the pay inequity she faced. A newspaper article inspired Susan Zimet to write this book.

We are all receivers, recorders, and makers of history. Reading about Anthony's vote, you may be inspired to look through local newspaper archives (probably online) for a woman who joined this massive civil disobedience campaign by voting, like Anthony, when it was illegal. Maybe you'll find a suffragist nobody knows about. The story's not complete; it never will be. There's always one more fact, one more forgotten feminist. Our choices impact the future, what we choose not to do as well as what we do. How much more quickly would women have gotten the vote if all the inactive women had joined the movement? How soon will women get pay equity and an Equal Rights Amendment? The answer is not in a textbook; it is in our actions.

I warned you. This book could change your life. Read it and then go out and make history!

—Sally Roesch Wagner, PhD and Founder and Executive Director of the Matilda Joslyn Gage Center for Social Justice Dialogue, in Fayetteville, New York

Introduction

SITTING IN A COFFEE SHOP ONE DAY, I CAME ACROSS A newspaper article about the hundredth anniversary of the fight for a woman's right to vote—a struggle also known as suffrage.

As I read, it struck me: I'm a woman and a former elected official, yet I knew so little about this enormous part of American history—my history. The struggle for suffrage wasn't covered when I was in school. No movies or books that I knew about told the story. I'd been politically active for most of my life, focusing passionately on women, children, the environment, and other social justice issues. Why didn't I know any of this?

My first foray into elected politics happened when I got involved in a fight to stop a mega-mall from being built in my small town of New Paltz in upstate New York. I ended up being asked to run for office. I didn't want to. I was working with Emmy Award–winning producers on a potential kids' television show and happily raising two children. But the pressure was unrelenting—and I really loved my town. So I agreed to run for town supervisor, which was essentially the town's mayor.

I was a new candidate, and the odds were stacked against me. But I worked and fought hard, and ended up winning. I was the first woman elected to the position of town supervisor in

New Paltz's history. On the night of the victory party, a woman I didn't know approached me and said, "Thank you for what you just did for every young girl in our town." Her words meant the world to me.

During my twenty-plus years as an elected official, I spoke with as many young girls' organizations as I could, hoping to teach and inspire them to break down any barriers that stood in their way. In this, as in so many other things, I was standing on the shoulders of the suffragists. I just didn't know it.

After reading that article, I was eager to learn more. I went to Seneca Falls and Rochester, New York, the birthplace of women's fight for suffrage. And as I stood in front of Susan B. Anthony's house, I found myself moved beyond anything I'd ever imagined. Because of women like Anthony, I could be who I am today. I thought about my childhood dream of being the first woman player in Major League Baseball. My dad had box seats at Yankee Stadium, right above the third-base line. I'd lie in bed at night after a game and imagine emerging from the dugout in my Yankees uniform to a standing ovation.

Many girls during Susan B. Anthony's time dreamed of nothing more than being born a boy instead. Back then, in 1800s America, girls were expected to marry by fifteen or sixteen, give birth to many children, and live by their husbands' rules: no matter what, he always had the final say. A married woman was legally her husband's property. Laws prohibited women from speaking in public or getting an education. If a woman inherited property, her husband could sell it and keep the money. If he beat her, she had no legal recourse. Women could not serve on juries, were denied access to many occupations and jobs, and, of course, did not have the right to vote.

The suffragists celebrated in this book overcame huge obstacles at significant personal cost to achieve their goals. And their legacy has given all American girls and women the right to representation and the right to have a voice and a vote, not to mention the chance to dream about being anything their hearts desire.

But there is still work to be done. The suffragists didn't just fight for the right to vote. They fought for equal pay for equal work, which we still don't have today. Too many single mothers live in poverty. Too many women still suffer domestic violence, sexual harassment, or smaller microaggressions and misogyny in the workplace. Even as town supervisor, I encountered unexpected sexism. When my first town budget didn't raise taxes, people said my husband must have worked out the numbers. One man told me I belonged in the kitchen, which is ironic, since my husband does all the cooking.

Remember these brave women when you turn eighteen and register to vote. Remember them when you proudly cast your ballot for every election, large or small. Consider running for office someday. You might just be the person who helps lift a child out of poverty, or gets a struggling senior the care they need. Maybe you will be the one to negotiate a peace deal that will keep our future sons and daughters safe.

We owe it to the women of this movement to know their names and learn their stories. To find inspiration in their fight and to honor them by continuing their work. Because it is not yet finished.

CHAPTER

Enough of the Everlasting No

The story of a woman's right to vote in the United States actually begins in England. And not at an event about women's rights at all, but at an antislavery convention instead. This story begins with a humiliating "no," and with a pivotal friendship born out of this shared, stinging, and all-too-familiar disappointment.

The World Anti-Slavery Convention of 1840 gathered in London on June 12, an unusually bright and sunny day. One month earlier on May 11, twenty-four-year-old Elizabeth Cady Stanton had boarded a ship called the *Montreal* with her new husband, Henry Stanton, to make the three-thousand-mile trip from New York to England, which would last eighteen days. Henry was a full-time abolitionist—a powerful speaker and leader in the American movement to end slavery—as well as a delegate to this convention.

Young Elizabeth was not a delegate and was still somewhat

new to the abolitionist movement and its ideas. But she was smart and well educated, especially for a woman at that time. A voracious reader, she spent much of that trip across the Atlantic plowing through books on slavery and discussing the subject with her fellow passengers. "Being the wife of a delegate," she said, "we all felt it important that I should be able to answer whatever questions I might be asked . . . on all phases of the slavery question."

Perhaps she studied slavery out of an obligation to her husband, but it was just as likely that she herself was deeply curious. After all, Stanton was, in some people's eyes, less than "ladylike." Passengers aboard the *Montreal* certainly took note that she called her husband "Henry" and not "Mr. Stanton," as

Elizabeth Cady Stanton with her daughter, Harriot, 1856. Harriot was the sixth of Stanton's seven children.

was customary back then. Elizabeth was assertive; she had demanded that she and Henry be married by a minister who would not force her to pledge to "obey" her husband, as tradition dictated. She kept her maiden name, Cady, announcing her determination that theirs would be a marriage of equals.

Even though Elizabeth wasn't a delegate to the convention, other American women were—seven in all. In the second half of the 1830s women had steadily grown more visible—and more vocal—in the American abolitionist movement. This didn't please everyone, and it led to major antislavery organizations splitting apart. Nevertheless, on June 12, 1840, male and female abolitionists together entered London's Freemasons' Hall to officially represent the American movement.

But only the men would be allowed to participate.

————⋅⊂⊗⊃⋅————

This was hardly the first time Elizabeth Cady Stanton witnessed the disadvantages of being female. Born in 1815 in Johnstown, New York, Stanton was one of eleven children, but she would be one of only five, all women, to make it to adulthood. Elizabeth was eleven when her last brother, Eleazar, died. She would forever remember finding her father, Daniel Cady, sitting in the dark parlor, "pale and immovable," by the casket. Entering the room, she climbed up on his knee. He put his arms around her, but then sighed, "Oh my daughter, I wish you were a boy!"

However much this must have hurt to hear, Elizabeth pledged to somehow replace her brother, to be everything

Eleazar no longer could be. Years later she wrote, "All that day and far into the night I pondered the problem of boyhood. I thought that the chief thing to be done in order to equal boys was to be learned and courageous." Elizabeth was already brave, and she would get a fine education, at least in terms of what was available to girls at this time. Despite demonstrating over and over that her mind was equal to that of even the brightest young man her age, she would not receive a true college education.

Elizabeth steadily came to realize that her goal of equality would not be so simple. Time and again, she would encounter the endless restrictions placed against girls, to the point that she summed up her own girlhood with these words: "Everything we like to do is a sin. . . . I am so tired of that everlasting no! no! no! At school, at home, everywhere it is *no!*"

Her father was a lawyer and later a judge, and as a child Elizabeth often overheard his conversations with women who came to him for legal counsel. Even if a woman was in a terrible marriage in which the husband spent their money on drinking, gambling, and other women, even if the man beat her, she could not leave him without losing claim to their children. Fathers held all legal rights.

Daniel Cady tried to help these women, but there was little he could do. When Elizabeth got upset, he showed her the relevant passages in his law books. Not only this; he told her that when she grew up she should "talk to the legislators; tell them all you have seen in this office—the sufferings of these Scotchwomen. . . . If you can persuade them to pass new laws, the old ones will be a dead letter."

KNOW YOUR RADICALS:

⁓ ANNE HUTCHINSON ⁓

The church claimed she worked for the devil. More than once, they put her on trial. Found guilty, Anne Hutchinson was banished from Massachusetts. Unfortunately, her suffering would hardly end there.

But who was Anne Hutchinson, and why was she viewed as such a threat?

America's first feminist, Anne Marbury Hutchinson was actually born in England in 1591. She lived—and died—more than a century before the United States was even founded. Like many early colonists, Anne and her husband, William, left for the New World in search of religious freedom. They were followers of the dynamic preacher John Cotton, who ran into trouble with the Church of England. Cotton left for Boston in 1633—the Hutchinsons would join him a year later.

In Boston, Hutchinson worked as a midwife, but soon began holding women-only meetings in her home, where she provided her own commentary on sermons. These meetings became so popular that men began attending. Eventually, growing numbers forced them to move to the local church.

At this time, women were offered a very limited education, with no chance of finding work that gave them meaningful power outside the home. Indeed, women were expected to obey men in every way. Wives were even considered their husbands' property. Not surprisingly, Hutchinson's strong, new voice was not welcomed by the male establishment.

Leaders in the community, including John Wilson, a senior pastor, and John Winthrop, a powerful politician, viewed Hutchinson's

An illustration of Anne Hutchinson's 1638 trial for heresy by artist Edward Austin Abbey, 1901.

sizable influence as a threat. Winthrop declared Hutchinson's meetings "a thing not tolerable nor comely in the sight of God nor fitting for your sex." He called Hutchinson an "instrument of Satan" and a witch "more bold than man."

By 1637 Winthrop was governor of the Massachusetts Bay Colony. Soon Hutchinson was arrested and brought to trial. Among other things, she was charged with slandering the ministers and disturbing the peace of the churches.

Hutchinson bravely told the men who sat in judgment of her: "You have no power over my body. Neither can you do me any harm, for I am in the hands of . . . my Savior. . . . Take heed how you proceed against me—for I know that . . . God will ruin you and . . . this whole state." In response, Hutchinson was banished from the colony, but a second trial was nevertheless held in 1638. She was again banished from the colony and excommunicated from the church as well.

After the trials, the Hutchinsons relocated to the more tolerant colony of Rhode Island. But when its founder, Roger Williams, died, they were forced to leave, out of fear that the Bay Colony would take over Rhode Island. The Hutchinsons moved to the Dutch colony of New Netherland, which is today part of New York City.

In New Netherland tensions between colonists and Native

American tribes in the area ran high. A war broke out in 1643, and the entire Hutchinson family—except for nine-year-old daughter Susanna, who was out picking berries—was massacred in their home.

Anne Hutchinson met a tragic fate because her courage to speak her mind led to her banishment and her eventual settlement in an unsafe area. But she has not been forgotten. In 1922, just two years after women won the right to vote, a statue of Anne and Susanna was placed in front of the State House in Boston. And in 1987, Massachusetts governor Michael Dukakis formally lifted the order of banishment enacted by Governor Winthrop 350 years earlier. Anne Hutchinson was finally allowed to come home.

—————◦◉◦—————

These memories could have come roaring back that June day in London. Because when the American delegation entered Freemasons' Hall, Elizabeth Cady Stanton and the rest of the American women, including the official female delegates, were informed they could not sit on the main floor. Instead, they were ushered to a separate gallery, where they sat behind a bar over which a curtain was hung. From here they could watch and listen to the convention, but they could not take part.

This decision to prevent women from participating became the focus of the convention's entire first day. Many men argued that such segregation was wrong, and some were even quick to point out the absurd injustice of treating women as lesser at an event calling for equal treatment of African Americans. Wendell Phillips, a prominent American abolitionist, said, "It is the custom . . . not to admit colored men into respectable society; and we have been told again and again that we are outraging the decencies of humanity when we permit colored men to sit by our side. When we have submitted to brickbats and the tar-tub and feathers in New England rather than yield to the custom prevalent there of not admitting colored brethren into our friendship, shall we yield to parallel custom or prejudice against women in Old England? We cannot yield this question if we would, for it is a matter of conscience."

Of course, the women present, now sitting behind that bar, were not allowed to contribute to the heated debate over their very place at the convention. When a vote was finally taken, an overwhelming majority of men supported their segregation. The American female delegates, no less devoted to the abolitionist movement than their male counterparts, and having traveled across an ocean, would remain little more than passive spectators.

How did Elizabeth Cady Stanton feel about seeing fellow American women excluded from participating, simply because they were female?

Stanton was, in her words, "humiliated and chagrined" by their treatment, especially at the hands of these men who seemed so moral before. She was stunned and outraged as well: "It was really pitiful to hear narrow-minded bigots, pretending to be teachers and leaders of men, so cruelly remanding their own mothers, with the rest of womankind, to absolute subjection."

But this understandable emotional response doesn't fully capture the effect this day had on her. Sitting behind that bar forever changed how she saw herself in the world. As one writer puts it: "With all the thinking she had done about slavery, liberty, and the American idea, it had never dawned on her until this moment: when the democracy was conceived, *she* was not what was had in mind."

All at once, Elizabeth Cady Stanton saw something she had never seen quite so clearly before: "In the eyes of the world I was not as I was in my own eyes, I was only a woman." And to be a woman in 1840 was to be less than a man. Socially less, politically less, and, perhaps most of all, legally less.

KNOW YOUR RADICALS:
◦ ABIGAIL ADAMS ◦

On October 25, 1764, a young woman named Abigail Smith married John Adams, a Harvard graduate pursuing a law career. John Adams would soon play a major role in what was to become the American Revolution, and eventually serve as the second president of the United States. But Abigail Adams would be no typical politician's wife.

Artist Benjamin Blyth's portrait of Abigail Adams at the time of her marriage to John Adams, circa 1766.

Women were almost completely controlled by the men in their lives at this time. After all, they were considered mere extensions of their husbands—just another piece of their property. Adams rejected this traditional arrangement and didn't keep her feelings a secret from her powerful husband.

In the years just before the revolution, John Adams spent much of his time in Philadelphia, far away from the family home in Massachusetts. So Abigail Adams ran the family farm and managed their finances. Like almost all girls back then, she had been denied a formal education, but her mother had taught her to read and write. This enabled her to correspond with her husband, and over the years they wrote more than a thousand letters to each other.

These letters demonstrate that theirs was a partnership of intellectual equals. He sought her advice on politics and government, and she was always ready to share her strong opinions. At times she offered suggestions he may not have been looking for. When she learned that independence would soon be declared, she wrote:

I long to hear that you have declared an independency. And, by the way, in the new code of laws which I suppose it will be necessary for you to make, I desire you would remember the ladies and be more generous and favorable to them than your ancestors. Do not put such unlimited power into the hands of the husbands. Remember, all men would be tyrants if they could. If particular care and attention is not paid to the ladies, we are determined to foment a rebellion, and will not hold ourselves bound by any laws in which we have no voice or representation.

John Adams, unfortunately, did not take this advice to heart. The Declaration of Independence would famously state that "all *men* are created equal," thereby denying women political rights in the new country. Nevertheless, Abigail Adams remained her husband's closest, most trusted adviser throughout his career, to the point that his opponents took to calling her "Mrs. President." Her desire for political equality between men and women would have to wait, but three-quarters of a century later, at the Seneca Falls Convention, her rebellion would begin, declared in language she herself would most certainly have approved of.

The only consolation here, and what a crucial consolation it would be, was Stanton sharing this experience with other women in Freemasons' Hall. Remember, seven female delegates from the United States had made that same trip across the ocean. These bold activists were used to lecturing to large groups, and it's hard to imagine that their disappointment was any less bitter than Stanton's.

Among these women was Lucretia Mott, a Quaker minister and accomplished speaker almost twice Stanton's age. Mott had been at the center of the controversies over the place of women in the American abolitionist movement during the last decade. The discrimination she suffered at the hands of the movement's men gradually convinced her that women's rights were "the most important question of my life." Long familiar with the hatred and cruelty sometimes directed at female abolitionists, Mott was less surprised than Stanton to be ushered behind that curtain. Never-

theless, the convention was a turning point for her as well. It seems that this insult was the straw that broke the camel's back. Her experience "unleashed her; thereafter she did not attempt to hold back either anger or commitment."

Stanton, for all her intelligence, boldness, and courage, had never before had a female role model, but she found one in Mott. And Mott welcomed her into a community of

Portrait of Lucretia Mott, 1841.

like-minded women. Though they had been silenced at Freemasons' Hall, at the boardinghouse on Queen Street where they stayed, these women "kept up a brisk fire morning, noon, and night," speaking their minds and confronting the very men who voted against their inclusion back at the convention.

Mott impressed Stanton most of all: "Calmly and skillfully Mrs. Mott parried all their attacks, now by her quiet humor turning the laugh on them, and then by her earnestness and dignity silencing their ridicule and sneers." Enamored with Mott, Stanton spent as much time with her as possible over the next few weeks. They walked the streets of London, talking about the place of women back in the United States, and became close friends. "I sought every opportunity to be at her side, and continually plied her with questions. . . . I felt a new born sense of dignity and freedom." For her part, Mott said of Stanton, "I love her now as belonging to us."

All this political talk was fairly new to Stanton, but still, she was unable to resist joining in the debates back at Queen Street. "The tantalizing tone of the conversation was too much for me to maintain silence," she said. Mott's subtle encouragement solidified her enthusiasm for this cause: "I shall never forget the look of recognition she gave me when she saw by my remarks that I fully comprehended the problem of woman's rights and wrongs."

It wasn't that Stanton had never considered the ideas voiced by Mott and the others, but hearing them spoken aloud and interacting with this community of thinkers and activists was a revelation for her. "It was intensely gratifying to hear all that, through years of doubt, I had dimly thought, so freely discussed by other women, some of them no older than myself." Three thousand miles from home, Stanton had found her intellectual and political family. With Mott as her mentor and with a new community to call her own, Stanton's vision for her future and the future of all American women came into focus.

So despite the profound humiliation they experienced on its first day, "the movement for woman's suffrage . . . may be dated from the World's Anti-Slavery Convention." Indeed, Stanton and Mott left Freemasons' Hall walking arm in arm, and resolved to hold a convention "as soon as we returned home, and form a society to advocate the rights of women."

And they would do just that.

But not for another eight years.

KNOW YOUR RADICALS:
ꙮ MARY WOLLSTONECRAFT ꙮ

"Freedom, even uncertain freedom, is dear," Mary Wollstonecraft wrote to her sisters in a letter. "You know I am not born to tread the beaten track." Wollstonecraft, born in England in 1759, could not have been more honest. She had highly unconventional ideas about how to make it in the world from the time she was a young adult, and the path she chose in life ran far from the beaten track.

Perhaps scarred by growing up in the home of an abusive father, Wollstonecraft looked for ways to live independently and settled on a rather risky career path: she would be a writer. To pursue her dream, Wollstonecraft moved to London, found work with a publisher, and got to know many great intellectuals, writers, and artists. She also began a relationship with a married man, but when this affair soured she moved to France.

In France, Wollstonecraft witnessed the French Revolution.

Inspired by the sight of common people asserting their power over a small, privileged ruling class, Wollstonecraft anonymously wrote *A Vindication of the Rights of Men*. This book advanced the importance of individual rights and was initially a great success. But when a second edition was printed with Wollstonecraft's name on the title page, the critics came after her. A woman writing a work like this was simply unacceptable back then.

An engraving of Mary Wollstonecraft by James Heath, circa 1797, and published between 1850 and 1870.

Refusing to be silenced, Wollstonecraft published a follow-up book in 1792, *A Vindication of the Rights of Woman*. In it, Wollstonecraft forcefully argued that women should receive the same education as men. Educated women, she wrote, were vital to society, since they were young children's main educators. More than this, she boldly claimed that as human beings, women deserved the same fundamental rights as men.

Wollstonecraft's private life was every bit as unconventional as her writing. She had love affairs and children out of wedlock, and attempted suicide more than once. After Wollstonecraft died at the age of thirty-eight from an infection she developed in childbirth, her widower wrote a memoir about her. He believed it was a compassionate book, but the scandalous details of Wollstonecraft's life shocked readers, and for a long, long time it was only her reputation, and not her brilliant writing, that the public cared about.

Fortunately, Wollstonecraft's writing was eventually rediscovered. Today *A Vindication of the Rights of Woman* is widely viewed as the foundational work of feminist philosophy, making Wollstonecraft the mother of feminism.

CHAPTER

2

A Leader Emerges and a Resolution Is Made

It's easy to say that for eight years—from 1840 to 1848—nothing much happened in our story. But a crucial transformation Elizabeth Cady Stanton experienced over the course of eleven days in 1848 grew straight out of those eight years, and neither this movement nor its leader would ever be the same again.

So much happened in London. The insult of the convention seating. The meeting of Lucretia Mott and Elizabeth Cady Stanton. Their resolution to hold a convention and form a society to advocate the rights of women "as soon as we returned home."

But "as soon as" was not to be.

Why? Why did 1840 turn to 1848 before such a convention would be held? And what happened in between?

The women didn't just forget. Indeed, Stanton and Mott saw each other again in 1841 and once more discussed the idea of a convention. Throughout these years Stanton read books on history, law, and politics, while Mott, in addition to her antislavery work, continued speaking on the rights of women. So why didn't they actually organize a convention?

It might be this simple: Stanton had been on vacation in London. Following her stay in London, she and Henry toured England, Ireland, and France for a few months. In Europe she could imagine all sorts of possibilities, including a convention for the rights of women, while the day-to-day demands of her life—as the new wife of Henry Stanton—were on hold. But when they returned to the United States, real life started up again—and pretty soon it got in the way.

For the first two years the Stantons lived with Elizabeth's parents back in Johnstown, New York. Her husband could not earn a living as an abolitionist, so he studied law with Elizabeth's father. Meanwhile, Stanton took advantage of the conveniences living in her childhood home offered. She read a great deal and participated in the occasional antislavery event, and these activities would prove important down the road. But for someone who would eventually lead the movement calling for women's independence, Stanton embodied something else at this time: dependence. "How rapidly one throws off all care and anxiety under the parental roof," she would later reflect.

In 1842 Stanton became a mother, and a year later the young family moved to Boston, where Henry believed the opportunities were better. Elizabeth Cady Stanton now found herself stuck, as she put it, in a "male marriage." Her husband built up his law career and pursued his political ambitions, while she managed the children—they would eventually have seven in all—along with the household. Though there were certainly other things on her always-active mind, Stanton took childcare very seriously: "Motherhood is the most important of all the professions, requiring more knowledge than any other department in human affairs."

Stanton knew that the problems facing women hadn't disappeared, but her own situation was pleasurable enough for them not to bother her much for a few years. In Boston she enjoyed a balance between her domestic, mothering duties inside the house and the social, intellectual possibilities beyond it. She was surrounded by a who's who of the leading reformers of the time from the abolitionism and temperance movements. There were plenty of fascinating people to meet, plenty of intriguing ideas to discuss, and plenty of stimulating events to attend. During her time in Boston, Stanton was wife and mother foremost, but she was never *only* these things.

As for Lucretia Mott, she kept up with the work she was already committed to before meeting Stanton in London. The 1840s were an intense decade for the abolitionist movement, and an activist of her stature would have had little free time to take on a brand-new project. Mott still believed strongly in the issue of women's rights, but she couldn't be the leader to advance the movement to its next stage.

In short, 1841 to 1846 weren't great years for the cause of women's rights. And for Elizabeth Cady Stanton personally, 1847 would be even worse. Though she was happy enough in Boston, her husband was not. That year, whether because of his failure to win political office or his lungs' poor response to Boston's damp air, the Stantons relocated to the village of Seneca Falls in up-state New York.

Soon the balance between dutiful homemaking and intellectual stimulation that Stanton had enjoyed in Boston fell apart. Seneca Falls was actually more bustling in the 1840s than it is today, but the remote village couldn't compete with their previous hometown.

If this weren't bad enough, her domestic duties only continued to grow. Their new house was larger, their children were greater in number, and she struggled to find good servants to help her. To make matters worse, all the children suffered from malaria while in Seneca Falls. Meanwhile, Henry traveled often and would be away from home for the birth of each of his seven children.

Elizabeth Cady Stanton was utterly consumed by her domestic duties. Consider this: before e-mail or texting, before the telephone even, writing a letter was just about the only

Elizabeth Cady Stanton with two of her five sons, Daniel and Henry, 1848.

way to communicate with someone far away. So people wrote a lot of letters back then. Throughout her life, Stanton was known as an enthusiastic and constant letter writer. And yet during the fourteen months from May 1847 to July 1848, she wrote only one letter. One. Stanton was overwhelmed, exhausted, and isolated.

Stanton later described this

period with these words: "The real struggle was upon me. My duties were too numerous and varied, and none sufficiently exhilarating or intellectual to bring into play my higher faculties. I suffered with mental hunger, which, like an empty stomach, is very depressing."

By the first half of 1848 Elizabeth Cady Stanton was hardly in a position to lead a revolution in the name of women's rights. But her situation reflected the place of women in general. Stanton was unable to work for women's rights, for changes that would enable women to advocate for themselves, because—in her "male marriage"—she was unable to advocate even for herself!

In other words, her personal situation was desperate, but it wasn't hers alone. She shared it with women all across the country.

———◦◦◦◦———

Elizabeth Cady Stanton's life was about to change in fundamental ways, and in this she wasn't alone. The year 1848 turned out to be one of historic transition, not just for women or Americans in general, but around the world. The French February Revolution replaced France's monarchy with an elected government, and a king was overthrown in Bavaria as well. Insurrections took place across Europe, in major capitals like Vienna, Prague, Berlin, and Budapest. Simply put, revolution was in the air.

Back home, a revolutionary legal change for every woman in New York, which had been debated by the state legislature for a dozen years, finally passed. The Married Women's Property Act prevented husbands from automatically claiming the right to any and all of their wives' possessions, and it became law in April 1848. The time was ripe for change.

To celebrate July 4 back then, Americans customarily read the Declaration of Independence aloud. In 1848 its bold words likely rang a bit louder than they had in previous years. Maybe this inspired Elizabeth Cady Stanton and the other women she'd soon work with.

Or maybe it was none of these things. Maybe it was just the fortunate timing of a friendly afternoon tea.

————◦◦◦◦————

Once again, Lucretia Mott would show up to play a pivotal role in Elizabeth Cady Stanton's life. Mott was visiting upstate New York from her home in Philadelphia and was to attend a tea party at the home of Richard and Jane Hunt. The Hunts lived in Waterloo, which is one town over from Seneca Falls. Mott asked Hunt if she would invite Stanton as well, and Hunt agreed.

On July 9, 1848, Stanton arrived at the Hunts' home to find six chairs arranged in the parlor. The chairs, along with a red velvet sofa, would be occupied by Stanton, Mott, Hunt, Martha Wright (Mott's sister), and Mary Ann M'Clintock, an abolitionist who worked closely with Mott. M'Clintock's two oldest daughters, Elizabeth and Mary Ann, may have been there as well.

What might Stanton have felt once she got there? Perhaps some relief. After all, she had managed to arrange a day away from home, away from her many tiring and monotonous obligations there. Perhaps some excitement, too, since she was going to see Lucretia Mott again.

But she almost certainly felt a bit awkward as well. She was something of an outsider among these women. Everyone but she was a Quaker and originally came from Philadelphia. Not only that—each of the other women at the tea was related to at least one other woman there, either by birth or by marriage. They already knew each other quite well. But other than Mott, it's possible Stanton had never even met any of the other women before. She likely dressed differently and would have addressed them as Mrs. this or Mrs. that, a term Quaker women avoided.

PUTTING IT IN PERSPECTIVE:
✎ QUAKERS ✎

Lucretia Mott, Susan B. Anthony, and some of the other key figures of the suffrage movement you'll meet later weren't just important leaders; they were all Quakers as well.

But what are Quakers, and why were so many of them involved in the fight to get women the vote?

Quakerism began when a group of Christians broke away from the Church of England about 350 years ago. They believed in removing everything between God and human beings. This meant, among other things, no priests. At Quaker services, which continue to this day, members gathered together, first sitting in silence and then speaking about their experience of the "Inner Light."

Also known as the Religious Society of Friends, Quakers were seen as a threat to the religious establishment and its connection to political power in England. After considerable persecution, many eventually emigrated to the new colonies across the Atlantic. But their numbers were never very large. In fact, today there are only around a hundred thousand Quakers throughout the United States.

So why were so many key suffragists Quakers?

Part of the answer is that Quakers were extremely involved in all the major reform movements in the United States in the nineteenth century, especially abolitionism. Believing that all people are created equal before God, Quakers were perhaps the first group of white people to reject slavery, and the list of important Quaker abolitionists runs long.

But there's another reason high numbers of Quaker women fought for suffrage. In Quaker communities, women have always been viewed as possessing the same spiritual power as men. From the very beginning of Quakerism women were allowed to speak at services. For this reason, educating girls as well as boys became a priority in Quaker communities. And these educated Quaker girls developed self-confidence and belief in their self-worth, which led them to reject the way women were treated in American society as a whole.

So it's no surprise that Quaker women would join the call for suffrage and be well represented among its leadership, though they made up just a tiny fraction of American women overall.

If Stanton hadn't come to the Hunts' tea, it would have been a very different, and probably forgettable, event. The Quaker women would have discussed the latest turmoil within their tight-knit community of reformers. But Stanton was there, and the course of history was about to change.

The tea didn't start with any lofty declarations. Instead, it started with Stanton, as we might say today, losing it. Despite being different, she was warmly received by the other women.

Next thing she knew, she had "poured out" her "long-accumulating discontent" with "vehemence and indignation." The women listened sympathetically as she described her struggles, but everyone there also understood that Stanton's situation, however difficult, was not hers alone. In this case, as in so many others, the personal was the political. Stanton's fate was the fate of so many women like her, not to mention the many more women without the means to hire servants to assist them.

Soon the women were discussing their rights—or lack thereof—with an intensity matching Stanton's. Perhaps she had already "stirred" herself, "as well as the rest of the party, to do and dare anything." Or maybe someone else deserves some of the credit here. Richard Hunt, according to Hunt family tradition, joined the tea party at some point and listened to the women's intense conversation. "Why don't you do something about it?" he eventually asked.

Whatever the case, the women decided then and there to organize a "public meeting for protest and discussion." Mott and Stanton's plan from eight years earlier would finally be realized! Normally, a date a few months in the future would be chosen for such an ambitious event, but the women knew they had to take advantage of Mott's visit to their area, since her well-known reputation and talent for public speaking would be their best bet to attract a large crowd. She was leaving soon. There wasn't much time.

Before their tea party was over, the women drafted the following announcement, which appeared in the *Seneca County Courier* on July 11 and a couple of other papers later that week:

WOMEN'S RIGHTS CONVENTION.—A Convention to discuss the social, civil, and religious condition and rights of woman, will be held in the Wesleyan Chapel, at Seneca Falls, N. Y., on Wednesday and Thursday, the 19th and 20th of July current; commencing at 10 o'clock A. M. During the first day the meeting will be exclusively for women, who are earnestly invited to attend. The public generally are invited to be present on the second day, when Lucretia Mott, of Philadelphia, and other ladies and gentlemen, will address the Convention.

Interestingly, the women didn't sign their announcement. Why? Because this wasn't about any individuals, and the women weren't interested in attention or credit for themselves. The convention was for women in general.

————•⊗•————

On Sunday, July 16, Stanton again took the train to Waterloo. It's unclear how or why she suddenly had the time and energy for all this activity outside of her household duties. Perhaps she was so inspired by the gathering of the previous week that she was now determined to do things she had recently thought impossible. Whatever the case, she traveled to the M'Clintocks' home to work on a declaration with Mary Ann—and perhaps some of her daughters, too. Stanton had already written a draft. They would write up a list of resolutions as well.

Stanton's first draft was okay, but it wasn't the kind of dramatic statement they were looking for. Luckily, perhaps because July 4 had been celebrated less than two weeks earlier, a copy of the Declaration of Independence was lying about. It may even have been on the round, three-legged mahogany tea table they would soon be writing on—a table that can be seen today at the Smithsonian National Museum of American History in Washington, D.C. Someone—Stanton never took credit for it—picked up the copy, read it aloud "with much spirit and emphasis," and suggested it as a model for their own declaration.

With only slight changes, this original, historic document served their needs perfectly. Consider the profound difference between:

> *We hold these truths to be self-evident; that all men are created equal.*

And:

> *We hold these truths to be self-evident; that all men and women are created equal.*

By adding a mere two words, the women had begun crafting a revolutionary document all their own, one that simultaneously imitated, altered, and challenged the founding document of their country's independence. This simple, ingenious move gave their Declaration of Sentiments—for that is what they called it—an instantly recognizable and memorable form. And though it was a radical addition, their revolutionary declaration unquestionably fit within an American tradition of justifiable rebellion.

But they weren't done yet. The women continued working

off the Declaration of Independence, replacing "King George" with "all men" in order to name the cause of their oppression and thereby craft a truly feminist statement. Their language pulled no punches: "The history of mankind is a history of re-peated injuries and usurpations on the part of man toward woman, having in direct object the establishment of an abso-lute tyranny over her."

Next, they came up with eighteen grievances to match the eighteen grievances in the original declaration. It required some time (along with help from some men), but eventually, as Stanton would later write, "we were rejoiced to find that we could make out as good a bill of impeachment against our sires and sons as they had against old King George." Last, they drafted a number of resolutions that would direct the discussion at the convention in a few days' time.

But once Stanton returned to Seneca Falls, she realized she wasn't quite done. Their announcement did not include the word "political." Maybe it was living all those years with a husband deeply devoted to the political process, maybe it was learning at a young age the way laws worked against women, or maybe all her pent-up ambition, now released, led her straight to a radical place others hadn't dared to go. Whatever the reason, Stanton drafted the ninth resolution: "Resolved, that it is the duty of the women of this country to secure to themselves their sacred right to the elective franchise."

The resolution, if approved, would demand for women the right to vote, a right no woman anywhere in the world, let alone the United States, had at this time.

By writing this sentence, Stanton transformed herself from a frustrated housewife to the leader of a revolutionary movement.

——❦——

Not surprisingly, those who found out about the ninth resolution before the convention were taken aback. Henry, Stanton's own husband, was "thunderstruck" when she showed it to him. Though "amazed at her daring," he made a bold declaration himself: he would not attend the convention. "You will turn the proceedings into a farce," he told her.

"I must declare the truth as I believe it to be," she responded, her newfound resolve on full display.

But Henry was not to be persuaded. He spent July 19 and 20 out of town, giving talks in the area. Her father reacted no better, threatening to disinherit her. Even her role model and closest ally, Lucretia Mott, was astounded. "Why Lizzie," she told her, "thee will make us ridiculous."

Despite these responses from husband, father, and friend, Stanton would not remove the resolution. As one scholar put it, "Once the idea of suffrage had occurred, and she'd seen it in all its dazzling rightness, nothing and no one could make her back down." It may seem obvious to us now, but she was the first to act on her understanding that only through the vote could women actually acquire the real power they would need to change their lives, and the country as a whole. "Depend upon it," she would soon write, "this is the point to attack."

But how would those at the convention respond? And would anyone even bother to show up?

PUTTING IT IN PERSPECTIVE:
ᴇᴄ ABOLITIONISM ᴇᴄ

As we saw from Lucretia Mott and Elizabeth Cady Stanton's experiences in London, the women's movement grew straight out of the abolitionist movement. Therefore it's worth spending a bit of time understanding this movement and its massive role in American history.

The term "abolitionism" comes from the verb "to abolish," which means "to formally put an end to something." So to "abolish" slavery just means to get rid of it. Because the slave trade predated the United States and sent slaves to many places throughout the world, there were abolitionists outside of this country well before 1776. To give just one example, Louis X had abolished slavery within the Kingdom of France way back in 1315.

But the abolitionist movement discussed in this book only started when English and American Quakers began openly questioning the morality of slavery in the 1680s. Once the United States gained independence, many steps were taken to outlaw slavery and the slave trade, but only in parts of the country. What followed then, for about fifty years, was a struggle over the future of slavery, in the United States and in newer territories (such as Missouri) that weren't yet official states.

The abolitionist movement Mott and Stanton joined was led by William Lloyd Garrison, who helped form the American Anti-Slavery Society in 1833. This organization included many free African Americans. Garrison opposed slavery because he believed the institution went against basic American values. He wrote:

I am a believer in that portion of the Declaration of American Independence in which it is set forth, as among self-evident truths, "that all men are created equal; that they are endowed by their Creator with certain inalienable rights; that among these are life, liberty, and the pursuit of happiness." Hence, I am an abolitionist.

Abolitionists wanted to put an end to slavery immediately, completely, and unconditionally. People who opposed slavery but were open to its gradual elimination—a group that included president Abraham Lincoln—were technically not abolitionists.

Many of those involved in the abolitionist movement were active in other reform movements, such as temperance, which sought to make alcohol illegal. But abolitionists were split when it came to the new women's movement; for instance, some supporters of abolition did not support women's suffrage.

As we all know, abolitionism would eventually realize its main goal, though this achievement would require the Civil War, which remains to this day the bloodiest war in American history. Abolitionism was inspired by a sense of justice, and was instrumental in ending the greatest form of injustice ever to exist in the United States. But the abolitionists weren't a reliable or constant ally of the women's movement, which sought to correct another terrible injustice. Sometimes the two causes were aligned, but sometimes—especially when short-term priorities got in the way—their members and leaders became bitter adversaries.

"At first we travelled quite alone ... but before we had gone many miles we came on other waggon-loads of women, bound in the same direction. As we reached different cross-roads we saw waggons coming from every part of the county, and long before we reached Seneca Falls we were a procession." These are the words of Charlotte Woodward, then nineteen years old, describing her journey to the convention. When her wagon finally reached the chapel, more than three hundred other people were there. This number included forty men, who would be allowed in, though they were asked not to speak until the second day.

Much to the organizers' relief, they had a crowd. But another pressing problem soon presented itself. The chapel was locked. So Stanton's young nephew climbed through a window and opened the door from the inside. People filed into the building, with its dusty windows and upstairs gallery on three sides. The first Women's Rights Convention was about to begin.

———◦◦◦———

In the days and hours leading up to July 19, Stanton had grown more and more terrified at the prospect of actually running this event, and of standing before all these people and presenting the documents they had prepared. She could count on one hand the number of times she had previously spoken in public, and she had never given a talk to so many people, let alone at a convention that she herself had organized and was responsible for.

But when she began speaking at eleven o'clock that morning something wonderful happened: she felt comfortable and fully qualified. In her opening speech she expressed how it was her "right and duty" to take up this cause. Women's rights were a woman's responsibility, because only a woman can "understand the height, the depth, the length, and the breadth of her own degradation." In addition to her speech, Stanton read the Declaration of Sentiments and then reread it paragraph by paragraph, so that those in attendance could respond and suggest changes.

The final document was ultimately crafted by all these women together, with an eye on the next day, when it would finally be voted upon. In heat that likely exceeded the ninety-degree temperature outside the chapel, the declaration was read once more at the afternoon session, along with the resolutions. The conversation was lively and serious. By now Stanton had fully found her voice, realizing she could defend her ideas with ease.

That evening, Mott—who had shared the stage with Stanton from time to time during the day—gave a talk on the state of reform work in general, a lecture that helped those seated before her understand how the cause of women's rights fit into a larger movement focused on equality for all. One person in attendance said of her speech that it was "one of the most eloquent, logical, and philosophical discourses which we ever listened to."

On July 20, the second day, the crowd was larger yet. So large that latecomers—like Amelia Bloomer, whom we'll meet again soon—could only find a seat upstairs.

As votes were going to be taken on this day, someone needed to chair—that is, preside over and run—the meeting. In a decision that revealed just how far women still had to go, the organizers decided it was unthinkable for a woman to chair, because men were going to actively participate. James Mott, Lucretia's husband, filled the role, and though this move might be seen as a blow to the women's claims, his presence and reputation gave the event an authority everyone recognized and respected.

During the morning session, Stanton again presented the declaration. After one last round of discussion, it was voted on and unanimously approved. At the afternoon session, the eleven resolutions would undergo the same process. All but one clearly had the crowd's enthusiastic support. The one that caused controversy? Number nine, the resolution Stanton wrote herself, the resolution calling for the right to vote.

Those opposing this resolution worried that such a radical statement would drive away support from the rest of the "more rational" demands. Defense of this crucial resolution came from a perhaps unlikely source: Frederick Douglass. Douglass, formerly enslaved and now a free man, was one of the leading voices in the abolitionist movement, and the founder of the *North Star*, the first newspaper published by an African American in the United States. He was also the only African American to attend the convention.

Douglass, who had run the announcement for the convention in his newspaper a few days earlier, spoke eloquently in support of the controversial ninth resolution. "The power to choose rulers and make laws" is "the right by which all others could be

secured." Douglass's "brilliant defense" of the resolution certainly pleased Stanton, but nevertheless, "he did not speak quite fast enough for me, nor say all I wanted said, and the first thing I knew I was on my feet defending the resolution, and in due time Douglass and I carried the whole convention."

Portrait of Frederick Douglass as a young man, circa 1840.

Carried, yes, but barely. In contrast to the declaration itself and the other resolutions, all of which passed unanimously, the ninth resolution was approved by a margin of only two. Nevertheless, it passed, and within just a few years this demand would become a central pillar of the entire women's rights movement. The unthinkable would soon go without saying.

KNOW YOUR RADICALS:
୶ THE GRIMKÉ SISTERS ୶

The whip cracked. Little Sarah Grimké heard the awful sound of leather tearing into flesh, followed by screams of pain.

This may not have been an unusual experience for a daughter of slave owners growing up in South Carolina in the final years of the 1700s. But Sarah would never accept it. From a young age she rejected the cruelty, brutality, and injustice of slavery. She treated the African American girl given to her as a servant as a playmate instead. She even taught her to read, though it was against South Carolina law.

In 1805, Angelina Grimké, the youngest of the fourteen Grimké children, was born. Thirteen years separated them, but Sarah and Angelina grew up to become best friends and lifelong activists.

In 1819 an unexpected trip to the Northeast brought Sarah, and later Angelina, into contact with leaders of the surging abolitionist movement. In the company of other like-minded individuals, the Grimkés found their passion, and their voice. As women who had witnessed the brutality of slavery firsthand, they could speak of its injustices in ways northerners could not. The Grimkés turned out to be talented, powerful lecturers.

By the 1830s, the Grimkés were in such high demand as speakers that men wanted to hear them, too. There was only one problem. As the Grimkés' popularity grew, some members of the clergy protested against their speaking to mixed audiences of men and women. These clergy members argued that, according to the Bible, God made women weak for their own protection. Soon churches were closing their doors to the sisters.

Rather than allowing themselves to be silenced, the Grimké sisters responded in anger. In an 1837 letter to fellow abolitionist Theodore Dwight Weld, Angelina wrote, "I must confess my womanhood is insulted, my moral feelings outraged when I reflect on these things." Their fight for the rights of African Americans forced them to acknowledge the limitations on their own rights as women. Angelina also wrote, "We are placed very unexpectedly in a very trying situation, in the forefront of an entirely new contest . . . a contest for the *rights* of *woman* as a moral, intelligent, and responsible being."

For the rest of their lives, the Grimké sisters fought for the rights

Engravings of Sarah (left) and Angelina Grimké, dates unknown.

of slaves *and* women. More than this, they publicly connected the two struggles. The two would face much opposition but had their victories as well. In 1838, Angelina became the first woman in American history to address a legislative body. Again and again the sisters asserted their right as women to speak out against the injustice of slavery. In doing so they paved the way for those women who would make the cause of women's rights their life's work.

One hundred people signed the Declaration of Sentiments, including thirty-two men and also young Charlotte Woodward. Seventy-two years later, in 1920, she would be the only surviving signer to see the day when women could actually vote.

In other words, there was still a long, long, long way to go. But a huge step had been taken. Elizabeth Cady Stanton, with the support and inspiration of Lucretia Mott and all these other women, had found her life's calling and would actively and fiercely dedicate herself to this cause for the rest of her life. As one historian puts it, "From 1848 on, Americans would be confronted with what Elizabeth Cady Stanton, never modest about the woman's rights movement, would call 'a rebellion such as the world had never before seen.'"

But as before, she wouldn't be able to lead alone. Soon she would cross paths with the woman who would lead the movement right alongside her for decades to come.

Her name? Susan B. Anthony.

CHAPTER

3

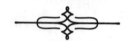

The Great Partnership

Elizabeth Cady Stanton was the first great leader to call for women's suffrage, but she would hardly be the last. In fact, only five years after Seneca Falls another woman—Susan B. Anthony—would join the cause with a devotion not even Stanton could match. Working side by side, these two very different women accomplished much more than either could have alone. Together they would shape an unstoppable national movement.

When the Seneca Falls Convention ended, its consequences were only beginning to ripple out over the rest of the United States. How would the country respond? Despite the convention's great success, Elizabeth Cady Stanton and the other organizers expected resistance beyond the walls of the Wesleyan Chapel. Indeed, the Declaration of Sentiments itself anticipated "misconception, misrepresentation, and ridicule." And it was right to. One newspaper called the convention "the most shocking and unnatural incident ever recorded in the history of womanity."

Another described it as "a most insane and ludicrous farce."

These papers and others like them opposed the cause of women's rights as a whole by arguing it would demoralize and degrade women. In the eyes of these editors, the traditional roles women held were the right ones: "A woman is nobody. A wife is everything." These editorials claimed that giving equal rights to women would lead to chaos and an immoral country.

But not all papers reacted in such knee-jerk, antagonistic fashion. In fact, a small but meaningful minority of newspapers came out in support of the convention. Douglass's *North Star* claimed that the event offered "brilliant talents and excellent dispositions," while another paper asserted that the female speakers demonstrated abilities surpassing those of the men in Congress.

The negative responses outweighed the positive, but to a certain extent this didn't matter. After all, barely three hundred people attended the actual convention. The country's newspapers, however, spread word of this event to thousands upon thousands more, to people who lived far away from Seneca Falls. In other words, the press provided the movement with priceless publicity. The call for equal rights, including the right to vote, was now something the American public would have to reckon with. Women's rights could no longer be ignored. This was a major victory for the movement.

As for the activists themselves, they were only getting started. Energized by the success at Seneca Falls, they decided to hold another convention just two weeks later. And this time it would be in a larger city: Rochester, New York. The Rochester Convention openly focused on women's political rights, and when it came time to vote on the ninth resolution from Seneca Falls, it passed by a much wider margin. Also, a woman chaired the Rochester Convention, something that still seemed so unthinkable that both Stanton and M'Clintock, who had ample experience with public events of this sort, at first opposed it. But Abigail Bush fulfilled her chair duties with ease, and the movement's momentum continued to build.

PUTTING IT IN PERSPECTIVE:
◦ BLOOMERS ◦

One day in the spring of 1851, Elizabeth Smith Miller, cousin to Elizabeth Cady Stanton, was working in her garden. Only something wasn't right. It wasn't the weather or the vegetables growing. No, it was her clothes. Quite uncomfortable in general, they were utterly impractical for physical activity of this sort. Like just about all women back then, Miller wore an elaborate outfit. It involved much more than the dress she wore. Under that dress was layer upon layer: petticoats, shirtsleeves, and a corset. The corset, often built in part out of whalebone, constricted women at the waist to create an exaggerated hourglass shape that actually compressed their internal organs. The entire cumbersome outfit weighed as much as fifteen pounds.

So what did Miller do? Copying a style she had seen while traveling through Europe, Miller shortened her outer dress to around knee length, removed most of the other layers, and added a pair of baggy, ankle-length Turkish pants. Suddenly she could move freely and enjoy her gardening.

Miller soon went to visit Stanton wearing her new outfit, and when her cousin saw it, she immediately adopted it as well. Stanton wasn't the only one taken by the innovation. Amelia Bloomer, a

The cover sheet of "Bloomer Waltz," composed by William Dessier in 1851, showing a woman wearing bloomers.

friend and neighbor of Stanton's who had attended the Seneca Falls Convention, started wearing the outfit, too. Not only this; she wrote enthusiastically about it in her newspaper, *The Lily.* The response amazed her. Hundreds of women wrote to the paper, asking for more information about the new look and begging for patterns so they could sew their own outfits. Circulation of *The Lily* jumped from five hundred to four thousand. And even though Amelia Bloomer credited Elizabeth Smith Miller with creating the fashion, the new look was dubbed "bloomers." By the end of that year Susan B. Anthony and Lucy Stone, a prominent suffragist we'll learn more about soon, joined in the bloomers craze, too.

But why should anyone care about a bunch of women switching from long dresses to short dresses and pants? Well, it was the first time in American history that women chose what to wear for themselves, without asking men for permission. And they chose comfort above all else. Switching to bloomers meant claiming control over their bodies.

In other words, bloomers were radical. Though some in the press supported the change, most attacked and mocked the outfit, calling bloomers masculine and tasteless. The larger public agreed. *Punch*, a popular British political magazine, printed cartoons portraying women in bloomers as beer-drinking cigar smokers employed in so-called "male" jobs, like driving a cab. Meanwhile, their husbands were shown in dresses, tending to their children. What began as a matter of fashion and practicality came to be viewed as a threat to gender roles.

For a while Stanton, Anthony, and Stone wore bloomers when appearing and speaking in public. They could make a political statement and avoid wearing a heavy dress that dragged in the mud all at the same time. But the harassment and ridicule over the bloomers were nonstop, and sometimes the criticism came from those closest to them. Stanton's children asked her not to wear bloomers when visiting them at school. One of her sisters simply refused to correspond with her.

Eventually, the activists concluded that the cost of wearing bloomers was just too high. Anthony believed deeply that dress reform was important, but not if it came at the expense of other goals: "The attention of my audience was fixed upon my clothes instead of my words. . . . To be successful a person must attempt but one reform at a time: By urging two, both are injured."

These progressive women reluctantly decided that not every righteous battle was in fact worth fighting. And just like that bloomers came and went.

———

In the audience at the Rochester Convention were the parents and two sisters of a twenty-eight year-old-woman named Susan B. Anthony, though she herself was not present. Anthony, a Quaker whose father strongly believed men and women were equals, was already a reformer activist in 1848. But Stanton's movement wasn't yet hers.

By working as a teacher and headmistress for much of the prior decade, Anthony had learned firsthand the value of her own independence, along with the limits even the most capable woman faced. As a teacher, she earned only one-fourth of what her male counterparts made. And once she became headmistress she could rise no further in her field. Frustrated by this professional discrimination, and with her father's encouragement and support, Anthony left education to become a full-time reformer.

The first question she had to confront was: which cause? Her childhood home was a vibrant center for abolitionist activism, but she chose the anti-alcohol temperance movement instead. Temperance was seen as a particularly good place for her talents and energy, since women suffered tremendously from the effects of alcohol abuse, which was widespread in those days. Many wives and mothers watched helplessly as their husbands drank away the entire family's earnings. According to law, money made by a wife or child had to be turned over to the husband and father. Women had no legal rights to challenge this or the beatings they often received when their drunk husbands returned home. For these reasons, the temperance movement was in many ways a movement for women's rights.

Anthony joined the Rochester Daughters of Temperance and soon became its president. In May 1851 she traveled to Seneca Falls to hear William Lloyd Garrison, the great abolitionist, give a speech. On a street corner after the lecture, Anthony was introduced to Stanton, who would fondly recall the meeting years later: "There she stood, with her good, earnest face and genial smile . . . the perfection of neatness and sobriety. I liked her thoroughly, and why I did not at once invite her home with

Susan B. Anthony at fifty years old, as captured by well-known photographer Matthew Brady, 1870.

me to dinner, I do not know." A historic partnership was about to begin, but before it could, Anthony would have to join the women's movement officially.

Though it wouldn't happen all at once, in the following years Anthony would experience the kind of eye-opening rejection Stanton had experienced back in London in 1840. First, in 1852, Anthony was elected as a delegate to the New York state temperance convention, only to be prevented from speaking by the chairman. A year later, at the Whole World's Temperance Convention in New York City, Anthony watched as the men in attendance spent three whole days debating whether women would be allowed to speak. In the end, they were not.

———✦———

What Anthony experienced, hardly for the first time in her life, was instance after instance of sexism. It was the same general sexism that Elizabeth Cady Stanton and Lucretia Mott endured in London in 1840. And the same sexism the Grimké sisters, Mary Wollstonecraft, Anne Hutchinson, and countless other women confronted again and again.

There are many definitions of "sexism," but all of them describe discrimination against a group of people—almost always women—based on their sex. Sexism is a prejudice that is often ingrained and institutionalized. And in nineteenth-century America the belief that men were superior to women ran very deep, so deep that most people—men *and* women—didn't think twice about it; they simply assumed that a society in which women had fewer rights than men was "just the way things are."

Put differently, sexism was so prevalent in the United States in 1852 that there wasn't even a word for it. Indeed, the word "sexism" wouldn't become widely used until the 1960s! But maybe that shouldn't come as such a surprise. After all, we don't have a term for living in a world in which gravity is always at work. Why would we? It's just the way things are.

But Susan B. Anthony refused to accept the way things were. In 1853 she left the temperance movement and joined forces with Elizabeth Cady Stanton to battle this thing so huge, so widespread, and so common it didn't even have a name. Their historic alliance would last more than half a century and change the United States forever.

———◦❀◦———

On the surface, the Stanton-Anthony partnership was an unlikely one. Stanton was married and would eventually have seven children. Anthony never married and never had children. Stanton was short and, by middle age, quite stout. Anthony was, in those times, a tall and angular five foot six. Their personalities and dispositions were quite different as well. Stanton was cheery, Anthony serious. Stanton was exuberant, Anthony quietly disciplined.

But their many dif-
ferences somehow fit to-
gether. In other words, the
two women complemented
each other perfectly, and
this was the secret to the
force of their great partnership. Together they
achieved much more than
either one could have ac-
complished alone. Stanton
was the movement's great
thinker, whereas Anthony
put this thought into ac-
tion. As Stanton wonder-
fully put it, "I forged the

*Elizabeth Cady Stanton (seated) and
Susan B. Anthony reviewing a speech, date
unknown.*

thunderbolts and she fired them." Elizabeth's husband, Henry,
described something similar: "You stir up Susan & she stirs the
world."

Stanton had, in Anthony's words, the "big brain," but even
when it came to writing, she relied on Anthony. Stanton explained their way of working like this:

> *In thought and sympathy we were as one, and in the di-
> vision of labor we exactly complemented each other. In writ-
> ing we did better work than either could alone. While she is
> slow and analytic in composition, I am rapid and synthetic.
> I am the better writer, she the better critic. She supplied the
> facts and statistics, I the philosophy and rhetoric.*

And just as important as the incredible way these two women's personalities and skills combined was the fierce devotion Anthony brought to the cause. In fact, no woman before Anthony had been as single-mindedly dedicated to the movement as she was. Much of this was made possible by her decision—and it was a decision—to remain unmarried; or, as she put it, to embrace her "single blessedness." She was quite blunt about the reason. "I would not object to marriage if it were not that women throw away every plan and purpose of their own life, to conform to the plans and purposes of a man's life."

It's fair to assume that every women's rights activist understood how the obligations of marriage and mothering took time and energy away from the cause, but many married and had children anyway. Anthony refused to do either and expressed her disappointment and even her feeling of betrayal about those who chose otherwise.

Anthony took the relative freedom she enjoyed as a single woman and used all of it to work for women's rights. To get a sense for just how intense her devotion was, consider the amount of traveling she did. During the many decades Anthony was active, the closest the average woman could come to making her political voice heard was by signing a petition. Thus there were endless petition campaigns. But in order to gather signatures, one had no choice but to go from city to city, town to town, and even door to door. It was slow, difficult, and often unrewarding work.

Nevertheless, Anthony, in addition to lecturing, organizing, and writing, gathered signatures year after year, marching through the snow, traveling in freezing railcars, and riding in backbreaking carriages. Few women traveled alone at that time, and hotels regularly refused her rooms. Still, she kept on. As one writer puts it, "In her fifty-six years of activism Susan B. Anthony probably traveled more than any other American." In fact, Anthony was on the road so often that she only established a permanent home in 1890, when she was already seventy years old.

Despite all the obstacles she confronted throughout her many years working for the movement, Anthony always maintained a quiet, steady optimism. It appeared she knew that history was on her side. As she famously put it near the end of her life, "With such women consecrating their lives—Failure is impossible."

PUTTING IT IN PERSPECTIVE:
๛ TERMINOLOGY ๛

Everyone knows what the word "vote" means, but two other central terms in this book might not be so familiar: "suffrage" and "franchise" (along with the related terms "suffragist," "enfranchise," and "enfranchisement"). What exactly do these strange-sounding words mean? Where did they come from? And how do you use them?

The word "suffrage" comes from the Latin word *suffragium*, which means "vote," "political support," or even "the right to vote." Though it sounds close, the word "suffrage" has no relationship to the word "suffering." An early appearance of "suffrage" in the English language can be found in the US Constitution, written in 1787. In Article V of the Constitution it is written that "no State, without its consent, shall be deprived of its equal suffrage in the Senate." Put differently, this phrase means that no state will be deprived of its equal right to vote in the Senate.

The term "universal suffrage" refers to the right of everyone to vote, regardless of race or sex. And a "suffragist" is a person who supports suffrage, especially for women. In England more radical female supporters of suffrage for women, whom we'll read about in chapter 6, came to be called "suffragettes."

The word "franchise" originally comes from French, where it means "freedom," "right," or "privilege." You might already be familiar with this term, because "franchise" is also used when talking about chain stores and restaurants. For instance, someone might say, "They opened a new McDonald's franchise down the street." But when it comes to voting, "franchise" has a slightly different application. Here it means a right or privilege, usually to vote, as granted by law. The phrase "to exercise the franchise" is a fancy way of saying "to vote." To "enfranchise" people is to give them the right to vote, and to "disenfranchise" people means just the opposite; that is, when people are denied the right to vote or are prevented from voting, they have been disenfranchised.

The movement would need a partnership this potent and a co-leader as devoted as Anthony if it was to endure and eventually overcome the resistance it would face for decades to come. The 1840s ended with great optimism, but the next fifteen years would provide more than their fair share of challenges.

Male opposition and negative coverage from newspapers were widespread. This was to be expected, but a separate resistance proved more disappointing: huge numbers of women kept their distance from the movement as well. Why, if women like Stanton and Anthony were championing their rights so passionately, did so many women remain indifferent?

Some women, unfortunately, simply disagreed with the message. They believed that their present position in society was appropriate; that they truly were inferior to men. But there were other, more concrete reasons as well. Most women in the United States were poorer than the movement's upper-middle-class leaders. They were struggling just to survive, and speeches from someone like Anthony declaring the need for better education and control of property just didn't seem relevant to their lives. Last but certainly not least, many women rightly feared conflict with their husbands, since in most marriages men had all the power.

But the biggest problem for the movement in the 1850s stemmed from the troubling political climate of the United States as a whole. The conflict over slavery was growing more and more intense, and the country seemed on the verge of breaking apart. And it soon would. Drawing attention to women's issues became harder and harder as the decade went by. Even among progressive reformers, almost all of whom supported movements like women's suffrage and temperance, there was a sense that all efforts must be devoted to abolitionism.

——◦◦◦◦——

The women's movement held a convention each year in the 1850s, an event that ensured coverage, controversy, and an expansion of the community. But in 1861, when the Civil War began, Stanton and Anthony reluctantly canceled the Woman's Rights Convention. More than this, they essentially decided to put the entire movement on hold and return to abolitionism. As Martha

Wright, a feminist and signer of the Declaration of Sentiments, put it, "The nation's whole heart and soul are engrossed in this momentous crisis.... It is useless to speak if nobody will listen."

In 1863, Stanton and Anthony, concerned they weren't contributing enough to the Union cause, founded the Women's Loyal National League (WLNL), which was to be "the first and only organization of women for the declared purpose of influencing politics." They focused their efforts on gathering signatures for a petition demanding the end of slavery. With the help of two thousand volunteers, they collected more than four hundred thousand signatures by the end of the war, making it the largest petition campaign in the nation's history up to that point.

Famed Union Army nurse Clara Barton, who went on to found the American Red Cross and was an ardent suffragist, circa 1865.

The campaign was instrumental in the passage of the Thirteenth Amendment, which ended slavery and which will be discussed more in chapter 4.

The Civil War was perhaps the darkest chapter in American history, but the conflict gave many women the opportunity to experience the kind of new roles the movement had been calling for all along. With men away fighting, women joined the workforce in unprecedented numbers, where they discovered an independence they were reluctant to give up once the war ended. In particular, fifteen thousand women served as nurses in the Union army. Their contributions hardly went unnoticed. As President Lincoln put it, "If all that has been said by orators and poets since the creation of the world in praise of women were applied to the women of America, it would not do them justice for their conduct during this war."

Stanton and Anthony made crucial strategic decisions during the war. They showed patience, but never lost sight of their long-term goal. In fact, some sources claim that Stanton and Anthony, using Elizabeth's husband Henry as their connection to the White House, got Lincoln to agree to a deal: they would stop demanding suffrage during the war if he would support their cause once it was over.

Sadly, of course, Lincoln was assassinated only five days after the war ended, so such an agreement, if it ever was made, never could be put into effect. Regardless, after the country was officially whole again, Stanton and Anthony went back to work. The United States was changing rapidly, so perhaps new opportunities for women's rights would present themselves and the reluctance of the previous decade would be forgotten.

Or perhaps things wouldn't work out quite so easily.

CHAPTER

4

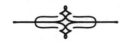

Postwar Turbulence

Stanton and Anthony made a strategic decision during the Civil War: they would place the women's movement on hold and put all their efforts behind the Union cause. They did this not only because it felt right, but also because they believed that once the war was over, they and their demands would finally be heard. If things were only so simple.

Just weeks after the end of the Civil War in May 1865, at a meeting of the American Anti-Slavery Society, the president of the organization, Wendell Phillips, gave his opening address. Though slavery had been abolished, he believed the society should stay together in order to win former slaves the right to vote. Phillips was a longtime ally of the women's movement. In fact, he had been at the World Anti-Slavery Convention in London back in 1840, where he bravely supported the participation of female delegates. Would he therefore now push for the enfranchisement of both women and African Americans? No. Instead he declared,

"We must take up but one question at a time, and this hour belongs exclusively to the negro."

Phillips's statement that women would have to wait their turn outraged Elizabeth Cady Stanton. Why had he suddenly turned his back on a cause he once supported? Phillips, along with many others like him, was not opposed to the *idea* of women's rights. Not at all. But in 1865 he viewed the fight for African American rights to be the most pressing and urgent task of the day.

The Confederacy had surrendered in April 1865. And the Thirteenth Amendment, which abolished slavery, had already passed in the Senate and the House of Representatives. It would be formally ratified in December of that year. But Phillips didn't believe this would be the end of the matter. In his opinion, simply abolishing slavery wouldn't be enough. Additional amendments would be required to guarantee civil and political rights for African Americans.

The idea that more amendments were needed was bad news for Stanton and Anthony. Phillips's strategy, which one might call practical or pragmatic, was based on the belief that passing additional amendments was going to be very difficult; the Civil War may have been over, but many political battles remained. And fighting for two groups at once—African Americans *and* women—was deemed foolish.

For decades abolitionists and the women's rights movement had worked closely together. Stanton, like so many others, believed their causes were fueled by a common aim: "The struggle of the last thirty years has not been merely on the black man as such, but on the broader ground of his humanity." In other words, if, as the Declaration of Sentiments stated, "all men and women are created equal," then giving one group priority over another was a great, unjust mistake.

Stanton couldn't believe that she and her movement were being repaid for their wartime loyalty in this way. A few days after Phillips's speech, she wrote to him, "May I ask just one question based on the apparent opposition in which you place the negro and the woman? My question is this: Do you believe the African race is composed entirely of men?" But she could not change his mind.

A conflict between the idealism of Stanton's side and the practicality represented by Phillips's camp was brewing and would prove irreparable. Postwar politics would drive abolitionism and the women's rights movement apart so forcefully that the women's movement itself would split in half.

And that might not have been the worst of it.

KNOW YOUR RADICALS:
◦ SOJOURNER TRUTH ◦

In 1851, at a women's rights convention in Akron, Ohio, an African American woman at least six feet tall rose to speak. She likely wore a white bonnet and a white neckerchief of the sort Quakers wore, though she herself was not a Quaker. She called herself Sojourner Truth.

She spoke: "That man over there says that women need to be helped into carriages, and lifted over ditches, and to have the best place everywhere. Nobody ever helps me into carriages, or over mud puddles, or gives me any best place! And ain't I a woman?"

Ain't I a woman? What did she mean? And who was this woman with such an unusual name?

Sojourner Truth, circa 1870.

Sojourner Truth was born Isabella Baumfree around 1797, though no one knows the exact year. For the first thirty years of her life, when she went by the name Belle, she was a slave in the state of New York. Before the age of thirteen Belle was bought and sold four times, and she would never be taught to read or write. The first man she loved, Robert, a fellow slave, was furiously beaten to death by his owner after he snuck out to see her one night. Belle was forced to marry another slave, Thomas, and together they had four children, though only their infant daughter, Sophia, would remain with Belle after she escaped to freedom in 1826.

In 1843 Belle changed her name to Sojourner Truth and became a traveling preacher. She recalled that decisive choice years later: "I left everything behind. I wa'n't goin' to keep nothin' of Egypt on me, an' so I went to the Lord an' asked him to give me a new name. And the Lord gave me Sojourner, because I was to travel up an' down the land, showin' the people their sins. . . . Afterward, I told the Lord I wanted another name, 'cause everybody else had two names. And the Lord gave me Truth, because I was to declare the truth to the people."

She traveled all over, speaking her truth about the horrors of slavery and all that she had endured, and meeting some of the most prominent abolitionists and suffragists of the time. At that event in Akron she continued: "Look at me! Look at my arm! I have plowed, and planted, and gathered into barns, and no man could head me! And ain't I a woman? I could work as much and eat as much as a man—when I could get it—and bear the lash as well! And ain't I a woman?"

Her Akron speech would become her most famous, even though it's unclear if it's exactly what she said that day. Since Truth was illiterate, she didn't write down her words. Two different versions, published more than ten years apart, exist, and one of them doesn't contain the phrase "Ain't I a woman" at all. Still, this is the version now associated with her speech on that day. But what does it mean? What was Truth getting at when she said, "I have borne thirteen children and seen most sold off into slavery, and when I cried out with my mother's grief, none but Jesus heard me—and aren't I a woman?"

Sojourner Truth with President Abraham Lincoln, circa 1893.

Truth was demanding that her listeners understand that women's rights weren't merely a matter for white women. Women's rights concerned all women, including slaves and ex-slaves. In fact, Truth herself only had five children, but her mother had thirteen, and by claiming her mother's suffering as her own, she was asking her audience to do the same. Women's rights, when looked at this way, were an inseparable part of human rights in general. It was a bold and powerful stance to take, one that rejected the difference between African American and white, woman and man, and even rich and poor.

Truth traveled and spoke publicly for years to come, calling for an end to slavery, championing the rights of all women, and courageously challenging a nation to no longer accept inequality of any kind.

———⋅∞⋅———

In May 1866, the Eleventh National Women's Rights Convention was held, the first since before the war. Many women, it turned out, were not going to give up on their cause so easily. They refused to see the current moment as a time to choose between African Americans and women. Instead, these activists founded a new organization, the American Equal Rights Association (AERA), which called for universal suffrage—for giving *everyone* the vote, African Americans and women alike. As Stanton put it, rather than people thinking about African Americans and women as separate, both should be "buried in the citizen."

Just a month after this encouraging development, the Fourteenth Amendment was proposed in Congress. While the Thirteenth Amendment had ended slavery, the Fourteenth aimed at securing African Americans "equal protection under the law." But it contained another, most alarming word: "male." The word did not appear anywhere else in the US Constitution or its amendments. It meant that a separate amendment would be required if women were to win the right to vote.

Stanton and Anthony were stunned. Anthony called the amendment "an outrage against women." Stanton expressed her fury in language that can only be viewed as racist. "As the celestial gate to civil rights," she wrote, "is slowly moving on its hinges," it was unfair that women were supposed to "stand aside and see 'Sambo' walk into the kingdom first."

Unfortunately, Stanton's use of "Sambo," a derogatory term for someone of African descent, wasn't an isolated incident. Writing about African American women, Stanton claimed, "Their emancipation is but another form of slavery," because "it is better to be the slave of an educated white man, than of a degraded, ignorant black one." When asked if she could accept African American men getting the vote before women, she answered similarly: "No; I would not trust him with all my rights; degraded, oppressed himself, he would be more despotic with the governing power than even our Saxon rulers are."

What are we to make of racist statements like these today? Some historians, while acknowledging Stanton's racism, argue that she should not be judged by modern standards. After all, views about African Americans and whites, even among progressive reformers, were radically different back then. Many educated Americans opposed to slavery didn't truly believe that African Americans and whites were created equal.

Though these historians have a point, it must be remembered that Elizabeth Cady Stanton wasn't just another educated, progressive American. She was a brilliant, bold, and idealistic visionary who was willing and able to express once-unthinkable thoughts time and again. To justify her racism as simply "commonplace" for her time ignores the fact that there was nothing commonplace about her at all. Stanton, one of the true heroes of this story, was deeply flawed and sadly wrong when it came to the matter of race.

And this pattern of racist behavior would continue.

KNOW YOUR RADICALS:
৶ LUCY STONE ৶

Lucy Stone was born on a farm in West Brookfield, Massachusetts, in 1818, the eighth of nine children. Although she was a faster learner than her brother, Lucy received no formal educational support. And higher education was out of the question.

Still, Lucy was determined. She spent almost ten years teaching to save enough money to pay for her own education. Finally, in 1843, at the age of twenty-five, she'd saved enough to enroll in Oberlin College in Ohio, the first college in America to admit female and African American students. Four years later, she became the first Massachusetts woman to earn a college degree.

Inspired by the writings of the Grimké sisters, Stone returned to Massachusetts and made her first speech on the topic of abolitionism. Her speaking skills were so impressive that less than a year later, in the fall of 1847, the American Anti-Slavery Society hired her to give speeches. Stone spoke on both abolition and women's rights. When the abolitionists felt she was spending too much time talking about women, Stone arranged to speak on abolitionism on the weekends and women's rights on weeknights.

Stone earned more than seven thousand dollars in three years by charging admission to her women's rights talks, a considerable amount of money at the time. One of her speeches had even helped convert Susan B. Anthony to the cause—and began a tumultuous relationship between the two that would span many years.

A young Lucy Stone, date unknown.

In 1850 Lucy Stone crossed paths with Henry Blackwell, a man seven years younger than her from a very prominent family. Over the next few years Blackwell grew smitten with Stone, but she wasn't interested. Stone told him that while she would be happy to be his friend, she would never marry. For women, marriage was like being a slave, she firmly announced. Eventually, however, she fell in love with him, too. Perhaps his profound dedication to the cause of women's rights—of all the men involved in the movement, he would prove to be the most committed—had something to do with it.

This didn't mean she was willing to marry. So for the next year, Blackwell reassured her that their marriage could work. At last, Stone agreed to become his wife—but only under a certain, crucial condition. Her identity, as Lucy Stone, was her life, and she was fiercely proud of it.

"A wife should no more take her husband's name," she wrote in a letter to him, "than he should hers. My name is my identity and must not be lost."

He answered: "I wish, as a husband, to renounce all the privileges which the law confers upon me, which are not strictly mutual. . . . Surely such a marriage will not degrade you, dearest."

And so when Lucy Stone married Henry Blackwell on a spring day in 1855, she remained Lucy Stone instead of becoming

Lucy Blackwell. This made her the first woman in American history to keep her name after marriage.

Susan B. Anthony, with whom Stone had grown close, cautioned Stone that marriage and family would prevent her from fully devoting herself to their cause. Anthony's firm warnings, especially against pregnancy, strained their relationship. But thanks to Stone's determination and the support of Blackwell and the rest of his family, Anthony's concerns proved largely unfounded.

As both a strategist and a thinker, Lucy Stone was much more conservative and pragmatic than Susan B. Anthony or Elizabeth Cady Stanton. In a long-term movement like suffrage, it remains an open question whether the radicals or the pragmatists are more effective. Pragmatists like Lucy Stone generally look at what's possible in the short term and make compromises in order to achieve a smaller set of goals. They team up with allies they don't agree with on every issue, and such alliances force the pragmatist to sacrifice certain goals. The pragmatist says, "A, B, and C are all important, but A is most important, so I'll give up on B and C for now." The radical, by contrast, refuses to sacrifice an objective simply because it seems more ambitious. She says, "A may be more important than B and C, but giving up on B and C betrays our ideals. We must fight for all three, even if B and C will be very difficult."

Even after she became estranged from Stanton and Anthony, Lucy Stone worked tirelessly for women's rights the rest of her life, often with Blackwell at her side. In the end they would be married for thirty-eight years. When Stone died in 1893, Blackwell honored her the best way he could, writing,

In behalf of the great principle of equality in marriage, I desire, in this hour of inexpressible bereavement, to say, with all the added

emphasis of a life-time's experience, that the Protest read and signed by Lucy Stone and myself on the first day of May, 1855, as a part of our nuptial ceremony, has been the key-note of our married life. After the lapse of more than thirty-eight happy years (how happy, I to-day more keenly realize than ever before), in her behalf and on my own, I wish to reaffirm that declaration.

——◦◉◦——

In 1867 AERA made a push to get women's suffrage into the New York State Constitution. Adding an amendment to a state constitution would allow women in that state to vote, even if the United States Constitution did not give them this right. Susan B. Anthony spoke on behalf of such an amendment. She powerfully expressed the universalist perspective, according to which all people should be enfranchised: "My right as a human being is as good as any other human being. If you have a right to vote at 21 years, then I have. All we ask is that you should let down the bars, and let us women and negroes in." Despite these words, their efforts failed.

Things were not looking good for the movement. But suddenly a new and utterly unexpected opportunity presented itself. Out in Kansas, the Republican-controlled state legislature proposed two constitutional amendments. One would allow women to vote; the other would do the same for African Americans. Both amendments would be voted on in a statewide referendum in November. If both were approved Kansas would become the first state in the nation with universal suffrage.

At first prospects looked good for both amendments. AERA sent Lucy Stone and her husband, Henry Blackwell, to Kansas in order to campaign, while Stanton and Anthony undertook a major petition drive back in New York. Though they occasionally encountered hostile opposition, they were more often met by large, enthusiastic audiences. But soon they realized that the two amendments, instead of bringing the causes together, were actually driving them apart. Once again, supporters of voting rights for African Americans viewed the women's cause as a threat to their own. By the end of the summer, Kansas Republicans, who controlled the state legislature, were not just supporting the amendment for African Americans; they were running an *anti-*female suffrage campaign as well.

Near the end of the summer, Stanton and Anthony came to Kansas to champion the amendment for women. The conditions were difficult: while Anthony remained in Lawrence, Kansas, Stanton went out on the road, where she endured fleas and bedbugs. And there was an even greater problem: without the support of the Republican establishment and with the campaign requiring more time and effort than expected, they found themselves running out of money. Desperately, they turned to a most unlikely ally: George Francis Train.

Train was a wealthy Democrat, a colorful maverick, a flashy dresser, and a complete and utter racist. His strong opposition to African American suffrage made the women's cause attractive to him, so he bankrolled Stanton and Anthony's campaign—he even traveled and appeared along with them. Train's very presence—one historian said that he "occupied a space somewhere between brilliance and insanity"—along with his willingness to publicly say the very nastiest things about African Americans, was enough to draw large crowds.

And crowds were what Stanton and Anthony badly needed.

Even though they were often idealists, Stanton and Anthony had made a practical decision in aligning with Train. They needed money and exposure. More than this, they looked at the showdown between African American and women's rights and decided to support their cause at any cost, using any means. As Stanton wrote, she was willing to "accept aid even from the devil himself."

But even Train's dubious help was not enough. In the end, both Kansas amendments failed to pass. If this were not bad enough, cracks were starting to form in the once-solid foundations of the women's movement.

PUTTING IT IN PERSPECTIVE:
RACISM AND SUFFRAGE

As we've seen, the women's rights movement grew directly out of abolitionism. Many of the women who eventually led the charge for women's suffrage called first for the end to slavery. It might seem like a belief in true equality, regardless of race or gender, ran deep throughout the suffrage movement. Unfortunately, the truth is that the women's movement was not free of racism, not by any means.

Why was this? How could someone demand equality between men and women and not see a similar need when it came to whites and African Americans? The short answer is that many advocates of women's suffrage were not free of racism themselves, though this attitude expressed itself in different ways.

Sometimes this racism was quite blatant, and stemmed from the fact that many white women believed that although slavery was wrong, whites were superior to African Americans. Holding both these beliefs seems impossible from today's perspective, but such a position was hardly unusual 150 years ago.

This racism was often strategic in nature, and this type of discrimination would surface in the movement again and again up through 1920. The white leadership, beginning with Susan B. Anthony, made a strategic choice to embrace, or at least not confront, racist advocates of women's suffrage, because their support was valuable to the overall cause.

In general, the South was less progressive than the North when it came to women's issues, meaning that winning support for women's suffrage was always going to be an uphill battle. Particularly if southerners suspected that the women's suffrage movement supported *universal* suffrage—that is, suffrage for everyone: male and female, African American and white.

Therefore many northern, white suffrage leaders did whatever they had to do to avoid challenging southern sensibilities. A clear instance of this came in 1895, when Frederick Douglass, who had supported women's suffrage since 1848 and spoken at suffrage events, was asked not to attend a convention in Atlanta. The reason was simple: his presence onstage might offend their southern hosts. There were similar incidents in the North as well, since racism was hardly limited to the South.

At times, suffragists working in the South actually argued that giving women the vote could strengthen white supremacy there. Starting in the late 1870s, so-called "Jim Crow" laws were passed throughout the South. These laws were intended to make it difficult, if not impossible, for African American men to vote. Some southern suffragists sought to gain support for their cause by assuring white voters that in practice women's suffrage would be limited to white women. Sadly, they weren't far from the truth. It would take until the 1960s, with the Civil Rights movement, to make suffrage truly universal throughout the United States. Even today voting suppression efforts targeting minorities continue.

———◦◌◦———

Back east, their longtime allies in the fight for women's suffrage saw Stanton and Anthony's decision about Train much differently. Lucy Stone and many others were outraged by their association with Train. In Stone's eyes, Stanton and Anthony had sullied their reputations and undermined the central aim of AERA. But this didn't stop Stanton and Anthony. After Kansas, they continued traveling and appearing with Train across the East and Midwest.

And things were about to get worse. The Fourteenth Amendment had been adopted in July 1868, and now the Fifteenth Amendment was fast following on its heels. The Fifteenth protected voting rights for African American men, in a sense reinforcing the Fourteenth. With money from Train, Anthony and Stanton had started a newspaper of their own, *The Revolution*. Stanton used its pages to speak out angrily against the Fifteenth, denouncing what she saw as an "aristocracy of sex" and once more calling into question who most deserved the right to vote. This time, in addition to African Americans, she demeaned the uneducated and immigrants as well:

> *The lower orders of men . . . the slave of yesterday are the lawmakers of today. . . . Think of Patrick and Sambo and Hans and Yung Tung, who do not know the difference be-*

tween a monarchy and a republic, who cannot read the Dec-
laration of Independence or Webster's spelling book, making
laws for . . . the daughters of Adams and Jefferson. . . . Shall
American statesmen . . . so amend their constitutions as to
make their wives and mothers the political inferiors of un-
lettered and unwashed ditch-diggers . . . fresh from the slave
plantations of the South?

Though her words seethed with racism, Stanton was arguing that it was unfair for poor, illiterate African American and immigrant men to vote when even well-educated women could not.

AERA held its third annual meeting in 1869 to discuss the Fifteenth Amendment and decide whether to support it officially. Stanton and Anthony opposed it, but many others, including Lucy Stone, supported it, believing they needed to continue working with Republicans and hope that women's turn would come after that of African Americans. The meeting was riddled with bickering and personal attacks, and it ended with Stanton and Anthony withdrawing from AERA entirely.

Soon after, they formed the National Woman Suffrage Association (NWSA), a much more radical organization in which no man was allowed to hold office. In response, Stone and her allies formed the American Woman Suffrage Association (AWSA). AERA was now dead. Worse than that, the women's movement, barely twenty years removed from that first inspirational convention in Seneca Falls, had split and would remain divided for more than two decades.

CHAPTER

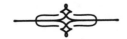

A Vote, a Trial, and the Long, Long Road to Suffrage

In 1872 Susan B. Anthony employed a bold tactic with hopes of proving that the law in fact already gave all women the right to vote. This led to her arrest and a trial. If her strategy proved futile, the women's movement would have no choice but to continue its slow, hard fight for suffrage, with the finish line nowhere in sight.

By 1869 Elizabeth Cady Stanton and Susan B. Anthony, along with a handful of other people around the country, had come to the conclusion that the law was in fact on their side. The Fourteenth Amendment—the same one that Stanton and Anthony so despised for including the word "male"—also contained language that could be seen as justifying their right to vote. The dreaded second section referred specifically to "male" rights, but the first section did not. It read, "All persons born or naturalized in the United States . . . are citizens. . . . No State shall make or enforce any law which shall abridge the privileges . . . of citizens."

Well, weren't women citizens? And if so, wasn't it illegal to "abridge"—that is, remove—any of their privileges, including the privilege to vote? And if that was the case, wasn't it *already* legal for women to vote?

Perhaps the current practice of not allowing women to vote was in fact illegal. To prove this, however, one would need a trial—a trial that would lead to a clear interpretation of the Fourteenth Amendment's first section.

Susan B. Anthony had a plan: she would vote. Not as an act of protest—not at all. She would vote in order to win the right for all women to vote.

Anthony started to put her plan into action on November 1, 1872, when she saw an ad in the Rochester newspaper encouraging people to register for the upcoming election. She, her three sisters, and eleven other women marched down to a local barbershop, where three registrars were at work. At first the young men ignored Anthony's demand and kindly insisted that the women leave. In response, Anthony read them the Fourteenth Amendment and threatened to sue if they continued to refuse. Anthony figured the registrars would stand by their refusal, which would allow her to have a trial.

But then came a surprise. Two out of the three men agreed, convinced perhaps by Anthony's promise to pay their fines if the government ever came after them.

"Well I have been & gone & done it!!" an excited Anthony wrote Stanton less than a week later. "Positively *voted* the Republican ticket—strait . . . 15 other women followed suit in this ward." Stanton wasn't the only one to learn of this. Anthony's act of voting would become a national news story.

And then Anthony waited.

Anthony wasn't expecting visitors on Thanksgiving a few weeks later when a knock came at her house at 17 Madison Street in Rochester. She opened the door to find a tall, nervous US marshal in high hat and gloves. Anthony invited him to come in from out of the cold.

Why was the marshal there? To arrest the fifty-two-year-old Anthony. His lengthy warrant read:

> *Without having a lawful right to vote in said election district the said Susan B. Anthony, being then and there a person of the female sex, as she, the said Susan B. Anthony, then and there well known contrary to the statute of the United States of America in such cases made and provided, and against the peace of the United States of America . . . did knowingly, wrongfully, and unlawfully vote.*

Her plan was working. He had come to arrest her for voting.

The marshal, clearly uncomfortable with the task that had brought him, politely told Anthony that the United States commissioner wished her to come by his office.

"Is this your usual method of serving a warrant?" Anthony asked, apparently amused by his timid behavior.

He told her she could report whenever it was convenient for her. There was no hurry, he reassured her.

"Oh, dear, no," Anthony said, "I much prefer to be taken, handcuffed if possible."

Leaving the embarrassed marshal in her parlor, Anthony went upstairs to change clothes. When she returned she extended her wrists toward him, but the marshal refused to handcuff her. The two rode downtown in a horse-drawn trolley. When the conductor asked Anthony to pay her fare, she responded loudly, so the other passengers could hear: "I am traveling at the expense of the federal government." She pointed at the marshal. "Ask him for my fare."

Anthony and the other women were charged with their crime in the same room where fugitive slaves had once been interrogated. All the women pleaded not guilty. More than that, they claimed they were victims of "political slavery." Bail was set at five hundred dollars per woman, the equivalent of almost ten thousand dollars today. Everyone paid, everyone except for Anthony. Instead, she applied for something called a "writ of habeas corpus," which would allow her to challenge the arrest, possibly before the US Supreme Court. The judge rejected her application and raised her bail to one thousand dollars. Anthony's lawyer paid the amount, and she was released.

This might have seemed like a generous act on the part of her lawyer, but Anthony wasn't happy about it at all. She asked him if he understood that by paying her bail they had lost the right to appear before the US Supreme Court to challenge the constitutionality of her arrest. "Yes," he told her, "but I could not see a lady I respected put in jail."

Nevertheless, Anthony would still have a local trial, and thus, perhaps, a chance to argue for her interpretation of the Constitution.

Anthony's trial was scheduled to begin more than six months later, in June 1873. Anthony spent the months leading up to it delivering a lecture titled "Is It a Crime for a Citizen of the United States to Vote?" She gave this talk in every one of Madison County's twenty-nine towns. So many people in her audiences were convinced by her reasoning that the prosecution had the case moved to nearby Ontario County. Otherwise, they feared, they would be unable to find any neutral jurors.

United States v. Susan B. Anthony began on June 17, 1873, in Canandaigua, New York. The case was heard before an all-white, all-male jury. Ward Hunt, recently appointed to the US Supreme Court, was the judge. The trial was expected to be a major event. Millard Fillmore, president of the United States from 1850 to 1853, was among those in attendance.

There was only one problem: Judge Hunt had no intention of allowing a real trial to take place. He wrote his decision *before* any of the evidence was even presented. Departing from the procedures of a normal trial, he didn't allow the defendant, Anthony, to testify. Hunt instructed the jury to find her guilty. Perhaps worst of all, he blocked the defense's request for an appeal so that they might have another, fairer trial.

It seemed as though Anthony's plan had backfired. Not only had she clearly lost the case; she hadn't even been allowed to argue for her position. But near the end of this ridiculous trial, Judge Hunt suddenly decided to do what any judge is supposed to do before sentencing. Ordering Anthony, the defendant, to stand, Hunt asked her, "Has the prisoner anything to say why sentence shall not be pronounced?"

Hunt would have to tell a defiant Anthony to sit down six separate times before she finished saying what she had to say.

Yes, your honor, I have many things to say; for in your ordered verdict of guilty you have trampled under foot ev-

ery vital principle of our government. My natural rights, my civil rights, my political rights, my judicial rights are all alike ignored. Robbed of the fundamental privilege of citizenship, I am degraded from the status of a citizen to that of a subject; and not only myself individually but all of my sex are, by your honor's verdict, doomed to political subjection under this so-called republican form of government.

Then came Hunt's first interruption. Anthony next protested the fact that she—like the American Colonialists before 1776—faced taxation without representation. Another interruption: "The Court cannot allow the prisoner to go on." Anthony then listed all her many "political sovereigns," all those many men who ruled her as a woman. Another interruption. She continued, drawing an analogy between women like her and onetime slaves, all of whom had to forcefully take their freedom in the face of unjust laws.

Back and forth they went until Hunt finally ran out of patience and declared, "The sentence of the Court is that you pay a fine of one hundred dollars and the costs of the prosecution."

Anthony responded, "I shall never pay a dollar of your unjust penalty." And she never did. But Hunt's decision not to enforce this sentence also prevented Anthony from appealing. *United States v. Susan B. Anthony* was over.

Anthony hardly achieved her main objective during this trial, but some good certainly came from it. First, she won in the court of public opinion by a landslide, giving the movement a great deal of very sympathetic publicity. Newspapers across the country viewed *United States v. Susan B. Anthony* as a mockery of the

American justice system. By harshly condemning the way Hunt ran the trial, many newspapers treated Anthony as she wanted to be treated all along: as a citizen first, and a woman second. With an eye on building off of this publicity, Anthony soon published and circulated widely transcripts of the court proceedings, titled *The Trial of Susan B. Anthony.*

Anthony was prevented from making a constitutional argument at her trial, but afterward a handful of other women across the country attempted to use the courts to prove that women already had the legal right to vote, thanks to the Fourteenth Amendment. One of these efforts, started by a woman in St. Louis named Virginia Minor, finally reached the United States Supreme Court in 1875, only to be soundly defeated. The justices refused to interpret the Constitution as the suffragists hoped they would. A once-promising strategy had reached a dead end.

Only two strategies now remained for the suffrage movement. First, convince each and every state legislature to change its constitution. Second, amend the United States Constitution. With Lucy Stone's AWSA working on the state-by-state strategy, Anthony and the NWSA focused on the second route, though she would spend much of the rest of her life traveling the country in support of the first, in part to continue spreading the word about their cause. Her goal was to get a sixteenth amendment added to the US Constitution, an amendment her loyal young followers took to calling the "Anthony Amendment."

Getting such an amendment passed would not be easy, since the process for amending the US Constitution is long and difficult. Not only must an amendment get at least two-thirds of the vote in both the House of Representatives and the Senate;

it must then be ratified (that is, approved) by *three-fourths* of all state legislatures.

Both organizations worked tirelessly for the next fifteen years to realize their respective strategies. During this time a new generation of suffragists joined the cause, many of whom had no memory of the conflicts that led to the movement splitting in half. Two such women, Rachel Foster Avery and Alice Stone Blackwell, Lucy Stone's daughter, again and again implored the older generation of leaders to work together. In 1890, the AWSA and NWSA finally put their differences behind them and unified to create the new National American Woman Suffrage Association (NAWSA).

KNOW YOUR RADICALS:
✺ VICTORIA WOODHULL ✺

If you think that a woman would have to be a little crazy—or at least very, very eccentric—to run for president in 1872, well, you'd be right. Victoria Woodhull was perhaps the single most colorful figure in the history of the women's movement.

In Ohio in 1838, Victoria Claflin was born to an illiterate mother and a small-time-criminal father. As a girl, Victoria claimed she could communicate with her three siblings who died in infancy. She also believed she had healing powers. So her father, never one to shy away from an easy buck, went into the healing business. He started a medicine show that traveled from town to town, selling elixirs and offering cures for everything from asthma to cancer. Victoria and her younger sister, Tennessee, worked as clairvoyants who, for a price, told fortunes and communicated with spirits.

Victoria married Canning Woodhull when she was only fifteen. She divorced and remarried before the age of thirty. In 1868 Victoria Woodhull and Tennessee moved to New York, where they worked as clairvoyants for Cornelius Vanderbilt, a railroad tycoon and one of the world's richest men. Vanderbilt gave the sisters stock tips that would net them $700,000, the equivalent of well over ten million dollars today. He also helped them set up the first female stockbroker firm on Wall Street.

The sisters used their new fortune to establish a weekly newspaper, *Woodhull and Claflin's Weekly*. In addition to covering financial news, the paper advocated for women's rights. It also devoted space to controversial topics, including sex education, short skirts, prostitution, and "free love," which, for Woodhull, meant that women should be held to the same sexual standards as men, and should thus be free to marry, divorce, and have children without government interference.

Woodhull's connections soon brought her into the realm of politics. In 1871 she addressed the House Judiciary Committee, where she argued for a woman's right to vote under the Fourteenth Amendment. This claim, which had already begun to surface among women's rights advocates in 1869, was the same argument that Susan B. Anthony would use to justify her effort to vote in 1872. Though the committee rejected her argument, many NWSA members, in Washington for a meeting, heard her speak and were thrilled. Woodhull was invited to speak to the NWSA and quickly became a central figure in the organization.

In 1872 Victoria Woodhull stunned everyone by running for president as the nominee of the recently formed (and, as it would turn out, short-lived) Equal Rights Party. Being a woman wasn't the only obstacle Woodhull faced. She was just thirty-four at the time, and the Constitution requires candidates to be at least thirty-five. But Woodhull didn't care about any of this. "If Congress refuse to listen to and grant what women ask," she wrote, "there is but one course left them to pursue . . . become the mothers of the future government." The Equal Rights Party nominated Frederick Douglass to be Woodhull's vice president, though the famous African

Victoria Woodhull, circa 1870.

American leader would never acknowledge this.

Woodhull the candidate was attacked by the media, which trashed her for everything from her support of free love to her "scruffy white-trash relatives." Despite this, Elizabeth Cady Stanton loyally supported her run. Susan B. Anthony, however, knew that Woodhull could not succeed and viewed her as a distraction liable to hurt the movement.

As the election approached, Woodhull's newspaper found itself in financial trouble. In response, *Woodhull and Claflin's Weekly* published a sensational story exposing an affair between Henry Ward Beecher, a well-known Protestant minister, and Elizabeth Tilton, the wife of one of his best friends and a devout parishioner. The affair became one of the great scandals of the nineteenth century.

Though it was published in part to save the paper, Woodhull

also saw the scandal as a great example of male hypocrisy. After all the criticism she had endured for speaking about free love, here was a revered religious figure committing adultery with a congregant. But Woodhull paid a great price for publishing this story. She was arrested for violating the Comstock Law, which prohibited the publication of sexually explicit material. She spent Election Day in jail.

In the end, Woodhull's name didn't even appear on the ballot in 1872. Her run would also mark the end of her participation in the struggle for suffrage. She moved to England in 1883, where she would remain until her death in 1927. Woodhull lived to see another woman run for US president—Belva Lockwood, candidate for the National Equal Rights Party in 1884 and 1888—and to see women finally get the vote in the both England and the United States.

———•———

While Anthony never stopped traveling, organizing, and training the next generation of suffragists, Elizabeth Cady Stanton gradually lost much of her excitement for activism. She found it harder and harder to muster the patience for long petition drives or tedious annual meetings. And more and more she refused to subject herself to the indignity of speaking before uninterested and sometimes rude legislators, nearly all of whom she viewed as her intellectual inferiors.

This doesn't mean that she lost her passion for the cause—not at all. Indeed, she grew even more radical, and the boldness of her thinking found its expression in her writing. In the final decades of her life, Elizabeth Cady Stanton fully devoted herself to articulating the deepest beliefs behind her activism, and in this way she became the great philosopher and ideologue of the women's movement. In fact, her work from this period reveals a concern with issues much larger than suffrage, however much she continued to believe in the vital importance of that central right.

In 1892, Stanton wrote what was to become her most famous essay, "The Solitude of the Self." This profound work understands women's independence not so much as something to aspire to, but rather as a simple, unavoidable fact. Stanton wrote, "No matter how much women prefer to lean, to be protected and supported, nor how much men desire to have them do so, they must make the voyage of life alone." Here Stanton calls on women to embrace self-reliance, to find the inner strength to face life alone, since everyone, man and woman alike, has no choice in the end but to do just that.

Always focused on concrete political change, Anthony did not care for the abstract philosophical concerns of this essay. Stanton, however, believed it to be her finest work, one that revealed the full significance of demanding equal rights for women. Regardless, Stanton wasn't done putting her radical opinions down on paper. In 1895 she published *The Woman's Bible*, which took direct aim at the religious establishment. This highly controversial work attacked the long-standing view—supposedly supported by the sacred text itself—that a woman was "an inferior being, subject to man."

Stanton's argument in *The Woman's Bible* was not only that this widespread view was the product of a selective and often inaccurate reading of the Bible; she went well past this, accusing the church of playing a central role in the centuries-long mistreatment of women by supporting this interpretation. Not surprisingly, *The Woman's Bible* was condemned by many as utterly blasphemous, as if Stanton herself had become the devil's personal spokeswoman.

Stanton was actually pleased with this response, since the intensity of the opposition reassured her that *The Woman's Bible* had shone light on a truth many powerful people wished to keep in the dark. Anthony, however, refused to help her, concerned that such a controversial project would draw negative attention to the larger movement. Nevertheless, when the NAWSA chose to censure the book at their annual convention in 1896 for being too controversial, it was Anthony who came to Stanton's defense, calling for the organization to respect one of its founding leaders and the inclusiveness for which she had stood for decades.

And so the two continued, more separate than together, all the way into the twentieth century. Overweight for years and now nearly blind, Stanton died at the age of eighty-six in 1902. But she kept writing until the end, dictating a letter to President Teddy Roosevelt the very week of her death, calling on him to endorse "the complete emancipation of women." When Anthony learned of her friend's passing, she simply said, "How lonesome do I feel."

For her part, Anthony carried on, giving all she had to the cause that was her life. She visited eighteen states between the time she officially stepped down from the leadership of the NAWSA in 1900 and her death six years later. Anthony planned on attending the organization's national convention in February 1906, but a bad cold prevented her from traveling. She died a month later, also at the age of eighty-six. Knowing full well that much work remained, she left her entire estate to the movement.

KNOW YOUR RADICALS:
ᢒᵌ MATILDA JOSLYN GAGE ᢒᵌ

Each and every woman working for a woman's right to vote had to ask herself: How radical will I be? Her answer determined everything else.

For instance, when it came to demands, would the activist call only for the right to vote, or would she insist on overturning all laws that discriminated against women? Would the activist draw attention to underlying sources of discrimination, or proceed as if getting the vote was all that mattered?

From an early age, Matilda Joslyn Gage chose to be the radical's radical, a woman who refused to compromise, even when everyone else around her was doing just that.

Like so many women in this book, Matilda Joslyn, born in 1826, was raised in a home of progressive reformers, where both parents believed in equality for all. Indeed, their home was actually a station on the famous Underground Railroad, created to help African American slaves escape to freedom.

Matilda herself benefited greatly from her father's conviction that a strong education was absolutely vital for all young people, including girls. Not only was Matilda sent to a good school; at home her father taught her additional subjects, such as math and anatomy. The two even dissected animals together, because Matilda dreamed of becoming a doctor.

But when she applied to Geneva Medical College, she was refused admission because she was a woman. Following this setback, Matilda turned to activism. Incidentally, just a few years later Elizabeth Blackwell, the sister-in-law of Lucy Stone and sister of Henry Blackwell, would be accepted, and would later graduate, making her the first female physician in the United States.

After marrying Henry Gage, Matilda Joslyn Gage turned their home into another stop on the Underground Railroad. In 1850, she risked imprisonment by signing a petition stating that she would not obey the Fugitive Slave Law, which prohibited any citizen of the United States from assisting slaves in their quest for freedom. She began writing articles and speeches in support of the temperance movement. And throughout this time, she continued learning. Fueled by an interest in theology, she taught herself Hebrew and Greek so that she could read the Bible in its original languages.

Gage attended her first women's rights gathering, the third National Women's Rights Convention, in 1852. She was only twenty-six years old, but she delivered her first major speech there. Though this was an event for women, she discussed the similarities between the limited rights of slaves and women in the United States.

Gage would remain involved in the women's rights movement for the rest of her life, often working closely with both Stanton and Anthony, despite their differences on abolitionism. She served as president of the NWSA from 1875 to 1876. When Stanton and Anthony decided to document the suffrage movement, they chose Gage (along with Ida Husted Harper) to be their coauthor.

Gage's radicalism found its expression in many ways. In 1871, she attempted to vote, a year before Anthony did. And when Anthony was arrested and brought to trial, *Matilda Joslyn Gage, circa 1870.*

Gage defended her at great length, arguing that both law and morality supported her effort to vote.

But perhaps Gage's most radical act would come in 1890, when the two main suffrage organizations, the NWSA and AWSA, finally merged back together into NAWSA. Gage, along with Stanton, would oppose the merger, once more choosing radicalism over compromise. Rather than joining the NAWSA, Gage would establish the Women's National Liberal Union, which she would lead until her death in 1898. In addition to supporting women's suffrage, this organization took more controversial positions, such as criticizing the male-dominated Christian church and its treatment of women.

Gage had, as we say today, the courage of her convictions. And when a younger generation of suffragists, led by Alice Paul and Lucy Burns, joined the movement a decade later, they would align themselves with this same radical tradition. In the end, their determined idealism would ultimately win the day, as the seemingly impossible turned out not to be so impossible after all.

———◦◉◦———

Among those thousands upon thousands of women Anthony trained and inspired—her "suffrage daughters," as she liked to call them—perhaps the most important would be Carrie Chapman Catt. Born in 1859 and raised in Iowa, Catt dreamed of being a doctor. Instead, she grew familiar with the limits placed on women and what it took to push beyond them. At college in Iowa she joined a students' literary group and fought for (and won) the right for women to speak at their meetings. A few years later she would become valedictorian of her graduating class, and its only female member. By 1885 she was the super-intendent of schools in Mason City, Iowa, the city's first female superintendent. She relocated to California and was soon San Francisco's first female reporter, but returned to Iowa in 1887 and began working for suffrage.

Catt had a knack for organizing on the ground and was a rising star in the movement by 1893. That year she was sent to Colorado to help with a suffrage referendum. There she created local orga-nizations and won key endorsements. Thanks to her leadership, the Colorado referendum unexpectedly passed, breaking a long streak of losing campaigns and making Colorado only the second state where women could vote (Wyoming had given women the right to vote back in 1869 when it was still a territory, in order to attract more women to the area and increase its population). In 1900 she became Antho-ny's handpicked successor to lead the NAWSA. Like Anthony, Catt would work tirelessly for the cause, traveling far and wide, and remain a central figure for many years to come. She would also, as we'll see, play a crucial role in the very final scene of this seventy-year-long drama.

Carrie Chapman Catt, circa 1914.

By the time Catt took over the leadership of the movement, there were

clear signs of progress to point to. Suffrage had more supporters than ever before. Congress regularly debated the merits of
suffrage and even voted on the Anthony Amendment from time
to time (though it was still far from passing). And four states—
Utah, Wyoming, Colorado, and Idaho—now had constitutions
that actually allowed women to vote. But despite these victories,
the turn of the twentieth century was not a great time for the
movement.

Why, you may be asking, did all this take so incredibly long?
Why was opposition to women's suffrage so difficult to over-
turn? How could so many people deny women this basic right
for so long?

These are complicated questions with many answers. Some
answers are so simple they're infuriating to consider: once
women got the right to vote, the size of the American voting public would double, and neither the Democratic nor the Republican
party was confident women would support it. As a result, powerful politicians viewed opening the voting booth to women as an
unnecessary risk. Politicians are driven by the demands of their
voters. Therefore, if a group of people can't vote, politicians can
easily ignore their demands. Women wanted the vote to make
their voices heard, but how could they do this without the ability
to vote?

This partly explains how Stanton and Anthony each devoted
a half century to winning suffrage and still didn't live to see the
day the vote was won. But two additional answers—one general,
one specific, and both more complicated—must be briefly inves-
tigated if we are to fully understand why this struggle lasted so
long and why its final years played out as they did.

The first, general answer points us back to our earlier discussion of sexism. Despite all their many positive qualities—intelligence, courage, stamina—Stanton and Anthony were viewed as being less than men and were therefore denied many of the rights and privileges that men enjoyed. But, of course, the treatment of suffrage leaders was hardly unusual in this regard. Sexism simply described how the country worked back then. This was the fate of each and every American woman, without exception.

When we consider this fundamental obstacle, we can see just how immense the struggle was. These women were fighting for more than just the right to vote; they were challenging the basic status of women in the United States. The specific goal was suffrage, but much more was at stake, and much more would need to be transformed for this goal to be reached. The very way people thought about women—at home, at work, in schools, and in government—had to change. And this change had to take place across America.

The kind of massive, nationwide change this movement was working toward could only be built out of countless tiny changes. Suffrage activists had to fight for every last one of these changes, and each one took time. In truth, considering that women still on average earn less than men for doing the same work, or the fact that only one out of every five US senators is a woman, it is clear that the larger struggle continues today.

The last, more specific answer relates to the crucial matter of strategy. The first couple of generations of suffragists identified and employed a number of effective tactics: they held meetings, started local organizations, held petition campaigns, published essays, and lectured to anyone willing to listen, including members of the government. These techniques spread awareness and turned radical ideas into acceptable positions. But as it would turn out, these methods would only get the movement so far.

By the end of the twentieth century's first decade, Carrie Chapman Catt and her followers found themselves in a strange position. On the one hand, not only did almost everyone know why women demanded suffrage; millions upon millions of Americans, both men and women, supported them. But on the other hand, the finish line was no closer. The movement had stalled, and the radical energy that fueled its early years had faded. For many people on both sides of the issue, the call for suffrage had become just part of the background noise of everyday life.

Catt was a compromiser at heart, a person who didn't like offending anyone. She often sought out partial solutions designed to fix things incrementally. This may explain her decision, as head of the NAWSA, to prioritize the state-by-state strategy rather than working toward a national amendment to win the vote all at once. But between 1897 and 1909 not a single state joined those four where women could already vote.

The movement needed a shot in the arm, a fresh, bold strategy that would force men in power to finally accept and act on the belief that American democracy belongs to men and women both. Thankfully a new leader, Alice Paul, would soon emerge to revitalize the call for the Anthony Amendment. But before she could do that, she would need to learn the revolutionary tactics that the movement so badly needed at this time. And to do so, she would have to travel to the place our story first began: England.

CHAPTER

British Tactics and New Leadership on Parade

While the American suffrage movement was still stalled in the early twentieth century, across the ocean a group of radical British "suffragettes" were using bold new tactics. Two young American women in London would join their cause, learn their strategies, and return to the United States to reenergize the American movement.

One November evening in 1907, Alice Paul decided to attend a lecture by a young British woman, Christabel Pankhurst. Paul, ambitious and intellectually curious from an early age, was raised in a Quaker home in New Jersey. She graduated first in her high school class and held degrees from Swarthmore College and the University of Pennsylvania by the age of twenty-two. She had traveled to England to continue her studies and pursue the field of social work, despite her misgivings about the limited changes she could make in that profession.

Christabel Pankhurst's subject that night was suffrage for

women, a topic Paul had only minor interest in at the time. But Paul never got to hear the actual lecture. Why? The mostly male crowd "completely shouted [Christabel] down." As Alice described it in a letter to her mother, they "sang, yelled, whistled, blew horns, played rattles etc from beginning to end."

Alice Paul may have only been an audience member, but she was smart enough (many of her instructors considered her brilliant) to see the similarities between Pankhurst and herself. Like Paul, Pankhurst was ladylike, well educated, and very ambitious. But despite her legal training, Pankhurst had been denied admittance to the English bar, meaning she couldn't practice law at all. And now, in a supposedly civil university setting, she could not even be listened to. Paul, who was considering an academic career for herself at this time because social work had indeed proved to have limitations, wondered if she would fare any better in that male-dominated world.

Despite this experience, Alice Paul didn't yet join the movement. But in June 1908, she decided to march in two suffrage processions. These carefully planned, colorful parades saw thousands of women winding through London's streets, making the cause newly visible to all those who had forgotten about it or who wanted to forget about it. The second parade—organized by the Women's Social and Political Union (WSPU), a group led by Christabel's mother, Emmeline—divided thirty thousand marchers into seven separate processions, all of which dramatically converged on Hyde Park, where hundreds of thousands joined a vibrant rally. Alice was thrilled to have participated.

But the march didn't change Paul's life all at once. Her decision to devote herself to the cause would stretch out over more than five years. She took dozens of small steps, gradually moving closer, until there was no turning back.

When Alice Paul finally did commit to the fight for suffrage, it would be with a single-mindedness perhaps even greater than Anthony's. Not only would Paul never marry, but from 1913 to 1920—the last seven years of our story, when she became the leader of the American movement—she would have no personal life whatsoever. Any friends she had were coworkers and fellow activists. Her entire existence was devoted to the movement.

Examples of Paul's fierce dedication are legendary. As a child, she was an avid reader of fiction, especially the works of Charles Dickens. But once she fully committed herself to suffrage as an adult, she concluded that reading novels was too much of an indulgence. So she kept her bedroom too cold for anything but sleeping. The mantelpiece in this same room was littered with small nicks. What caused them? The clothes she hung there because she refused to waste time returning outfits to her closet.

Alice Paul would not merely lead the women's movement in a few years' time; she would live and breathe it, working harder than anyone else and sacrificing every other part of her life for its goals. As one journalist wrote about her in 1919, "There is no Alice Paul. There is suffrage. She leads by being . . . her cause."

———⚬❀⚬———

Paul's training took place in England, under the guidance of the Pankhursts and the WSPU. As with their American counterparts, the Pankhursts' patience had been tried time and time again throughout the first years of the twentieth century. Their frustration with the slow progress they were making toward their ultimate goal was endless. By the time Alice Paul crossed paths with these British women in 1907, they were responding quite differently from their fellow activists back in the United States.

To put it simply, the Pankhursts were done playing nice. The old tactics of public speaking, gathering petitions, and politely requesting to meet with politicians (requests that were almost always denied) were clearly not working. Those in power mostly ignored the suffrage movement, so the Pankhursts chose a more confrontational route, to make this impossible. They started heckling candidates and interrupting speeches. They threw stones, broke windows, and cut telegraph wires. And when that didn't work, they spit at and slapped policemen, knowing that this would lead to arrest—and thus more attention for their cause.

The Pankhursts asked Alice Paul, who had proved herself by doing things like selling papers for the organization in the streets of London, to participate in a dramatic action to be held on June 29, 1909, an action that might lead to her arrest. Paul had never been arrested before, and was well aware that a showdown with the police was much more serious than simply marching in a parade. She wrote a letter saying she would be there on the twenty-ninth, but mailing it was another matter entirely. As she recalled later on, "I remember hesitating the longest time . . . and not being able to get enough courage to post

Alice Paul, circa 1918.

it and going up and walking around the post office, wondering whether I dare put this in. At last I got up enough courage to post my letter, saying I would go." If there was a single turning point in Paul's life, this was it.

On the evening of the twenty-ninth, before a crowd of fifty thousand, the Pankhursts sent sixteen groups of women to demand a meeting with the British prime minister, H. H. Asquith. These deputations, marching one after the other and wearing padding under their clothes for protection, advanced toward the Parliament building until they reached a massive police barricade. Told that the prime minister refused to meet with them and that they should turn back, the women did just the opposite, attempting to physically force their way into the building. Paul describes what happened next:

> *The suffragettes threw themselves against the lines of police & forced their way through once or twice only to be captured in a few minutes. Behind them was the crowd yelling & shouting & pushing them on but afraid to take any part for fear of being arrested. The police grabbed the suffragettes by the throats & threw them flat on their backs over & over again.*

Paul herself was arrested for the first (but by no means last) time that evening. Later that night, in a London police station among the dozens of other arrested suffragettes, she noticed a woman wearing an American flag pin in her lapel, so Alice approached and introduced herself. The woman was Lucy Burns, another bright, ambitious American studying in England who had gotten swept up in the excitement of the Pankhursts' new tactics. Paul and Burns spoke at length in the middle of all that tumult in the police station, sharing their suffrage experiences in England and their hopes for the movement back home.

Over the next eighteen months, during their crucial apprenticeship with the Pankhursts, Paul and Burns would grow incredibly close. And in the coming years these two young women would become the Stanton and Anthony of their generation. They worked together side by side during the final years of this monumental fight, making sacrifices and taking risks that even Stanton and Anthony had avoided. In this way, Paul and Burns renewed and intensified the radicalness that fueled the Stanton-Anthony partnership.

Like Stanton and Anthony before them, Alice Paul and Lucy Burns became an unstoppable team thanks to the way their considerable differences fit perfectly together. Paul was intense and unrelenting, whereas Burns was friendly and open to compromise. As one historian puts it, "Paul was the militant; Burns, the diplomat." The warmth of Burns's personality could help soften the force of the endless demands Paul unapologetically placed on everyone in the movement. These differences, of course, were overshadowed by their shared passion for their cause, to the point that they were often described as having "one mind and spirit."

Despite the strength of their relationship, it should be mentioned that Paul and Burns's partnership, unlike that of Stanton and Anthony, wasn't quite one of equals. Due to her exceptional ambition, boundless dedication, and willing acceptance of complete self-sacrifice, Paul would be the ultimate leader. Burns

Lucy Burns, circa 1913.

would spend more time in prison than any other suffragist, but unlike Paul she would also take breaks from time to time. Paul only slowed down when her health—forever compromised by the hunger strikes and force-feedings we'll soon learn about—deteriorated and she found herself in the hospital. She continued fighting for women's rights until her death in 1977 at age ninety-two. Burns, however, retired from political life altogether.

A month after they met, both Alice Paul and Lucy Burns were arrested again. This time the two were actually sent to prison. But even in prison they and the other activists found ways to resist, refusing to wear a prison uniform or even eat. This last tactic, called hunger striking, brought a great deal of sympathetic attention to the women's cause, and made the government appear brutal. After five days of fasting the women were set free.

Paul would spend the rest of 1909 in Great Britain, much of it alongside Burns, as the two traveled with Emmeline Pankhurst on a speaking tour throughout Scotland. They organized events, publicized the cause however they could, and, most importantly, observed firsthand the secrets of effective, radical leadership. And yes, they were arrested again and again.

In November 1909, Paul served a full thirty-day sentence.

Once more she went on a hunger strike, but by now the British authorities were responding differently to suffragists who refused to eat. Rather than allow a prisoner to go free for fear of letting her starve, the jailers introduced a new tactic of their own: force-feeding. Paul describes the horrific process, which was essentially a form of torture, in gruesome detail:

> *One of the doctors stood behind & pulled my head back till it was parallel with the ground. He held it in this position by means of a towel drawn tightly around the throat & when I tried to move, he drew the towel so tight that it compressed the windpipe & made it almost impossible to breathe—with his other hand he held my chin in a rigid position. Then the other doctor put the tube down through the nostril. When they have finally secured you in this position you can scarcely budge.*

The tube would rarely go in correctly the first time, and sometimes it would take a half-dozen tries before it did. Once in place, the doctors would pour a mixture of milk and eggs down the tube. Paul was "fed" like this twice a day for nearly a month, permanently damaging her health. In the years to come, Burns and many other activists would worry that Paul—often appearing frail and gaunt—wasn't physically up to the demands of her endless activism. But even when her health finally forced her off her feet, she continued working from bed.

———◦◦◦———

Alice Paul, still only twenty-five years old, returned to the United States in early 1910. Lucy Burns would remain in England for another two years to continue her work with the Pankhursts and the WSPU. Paul began establishing herself in the American suffrage community, mainly by giving talks, but she also returned to her studies and earned a PhD in sociology at the University of Pennsylvania. Despite all she had been through, she was still considering an academic career.

The American movement that greeted Paul upon her return was large, but it was failing to make meaningful change. In 1904, Carrie Chapman Catt had stepped down as head of the NAWSA in order to care for her ailing husband. Anna Howard Shaw, a physician and minister, replaced Catt. But Shaw, for all her dedication, was an ineffective leader. By 1910 the NAWSA had one hundred thousand members, but the organization had grown stale by failing to evolve. It was still employing the tactics established by Stanton, Anthony, and Stone: holding meetings, giving lectures, and collecting signatures. Once radical acts, these methods were now anything but. In short, progress was stalled. Fourteen years had passed since any state had given women the right to vote—yet the state-by-state strategy was the organization's main focus at this time.

In 1912 Lucy Burns returned to the United States. She and Paul met and concluded, much like Anthony before them, that a national, not a state-by-state, strategy was the way to go. They wanted to work for an amendment. Paul and Burns offered to join the NAWSA's Congressional Committee (CC), which was the arm of the NAWSA designated to push for a national amendment in Washington. Paul became chair of the CC, but this committee was essentially lifeless. Indeed, the CC had an annual budget of only ten dollars. Worse than that, the previous chair had returned some of it, unused, at the end of the previous year.

But Paul and Burns had an idea to change all this, and soon. They would hold a parade in Washington, D.C.

———⟨∞⟩———

Back in 1912, women marching, especially without men, was a radical act. Marching was associated with armies, and armies, of course, were male. Such a parade would thus challenge the notion of what it meant to be "ladylike," along with people's beliefs about the literal place of women in society. A well-organized, disciplined women's procession would demonstrate the determination of the movement and make people think twice when they assumed that power belonged only to men.

In addition, a large parade, back in the days before the Internet and even television, was as good a way as any to get exposure. Paul and Burns had learned this firsthand back in England. Done right, such an event could make a powerful impression. The two had learned more than a thing or two about street theater from the Pankhursts, and Paul in particular was, as one historian puts it, a "master of spectacle."

And there would be a special, key ingredient to this spectacle: on March 3, 1913, Woodrow Wilson would be inaugurated as the twenty-eighth president of the United States in Washington following a parade from which women were barred entirely. Thousands upon thousands of people would be in town for the event; Wilson was a native of nearby Virginia, so the crowds would be even larger than normal. For this reason, Paul and Burns decided to hold their parade on March 2. The bigger the crowd, the bigger the spectacle, the larger the exposure.

It was a great plan. The only problems? They had no budget and barely three months to prepare.

Despite these challenges, the two dove right in. Paul, who would prove to be a master fund-raiser over the years, raised $1,351 in the first ten days alone, the equivalent of more than $30,000 today. Marchers from all over were aggressively recruited and meticulously organized. Volunteers were brought into the Washington, D.C., office, which became a site of intense, nonstop activity. Paul, in particular, began working (at the desk that once belonged to Susan B. Anthony) with the kind of tireless dedication she would become famous for, leading by inspirational example.

———◦❀◦———

When Woodrow Wilson arrived by train at Washington's Union Station on March 2 expecting to be greeted by a large crowd, he instead looked around in confusion and asked, "Where are the people?"

"Oh," he was told, "they are out watching the suffrage parade."

Just as Paul and Burns had envisioned, the strategically planned event stole Wilson's thunder, seizing the attention of all those in town for his inauguration. A quarter of a million people witnessed eight thousand women marching. The parade was led by the stunning Inez Milholland, a prominent suffrage activist, who sat atop a white horse wearing all white herself, along with a crown and cape. The other participants— instructed by Paul "to march steadily in a dignified manner"— were divided into seven sections, and all walked behind a giant yellow banner that read, "We Demand an Amendment to the

Constitution of the United States Enfranchising the Women of This Country." The parade was an elaborate event, but its ultimate message was simple and straightforward.

The procession actually told a story, starting with floats in the first section representing those countries where women

Inez Milholland leading the suffragist march in Washington, D.C., March 2, 1913.

already could vote. The next section narrated the struggle of American women from 1840 to 1913. On and on it went, a vast, colorful procession made up of working women, state delegations, bands, and chariots, all of it parading along the very path that Wilson would take the following day.

But the parade was not without incident. First came the sticky matter of how, if at all, to include African American marchers. During the early days of organizing the event, Alice Paul supported and actively invited all suffragists to come. But over time, and under pressure from those fearing a backlash from white Southern suffrage activists and their representatives in Congress, Paul began quietly discouraging African American suffrage groups from participating in the planned march.

Nevertheless, on the morning of the parade, instructions came from the head Illinois delegate that Ida B. Wells, a prominent African American journalist and civil rights leader, would not be allowed to march with the rest of the Illinois delegation,

who were white. Wells was told to march in the separate, seg-
regated section at the back of the parade. She refused and apparently left altogether. After the parade began, she reappeared
and defiantly slipped into the Illinois delegation. From Howard
University, members of the newly formed sorority, Delta Sigma
Theta, also defied Paul's request. Together with their mentor, the
prominent African American suffragist-activist Mary Church
Terrell, these twenty-two young college women marched proudly
behind their banner.

The organizers had succeeded in gathering an enormous
crowd, but that didn't mean those lining the streets were supporters. Many of the men who showed up did so in order to
ridicule and harass the women. The boundary between the spectators and the marchers quickly disappeared, as did most of the
police who were responsible for maintaining order. The carefully
arranged marchers were squeezed together until their forward
progress came to a halt.

The men began to taunt the women, showering obscenity after obscenity upon them. They spat and threw lit cigars at the
marchers, who were also pinched, pushed, tripped, groped, and
slapped. The police were grossly outnumbered, a fact not helped
by all those officers who looked on with amused satisfaction. A
parade designed so women could symbolically claim the streets
of the nation's capital for themselves had turned into a very real
struggle for every last inch of pavement. The female marchers
used all the resources available to them—cars, horses, signs,
poles—to clear the way and continue forward. In some cases they
had only themselves. As one woman remembered, "Dignity was
about the only weapon we had."

The chief of police eventually called in federal cavalry troops from nearby Fort Myer to restore order; they took over an hour to arrive. Ambulances came and went, and they too had to fight through the crowd. In the end, three hundred marchers were injured, a third of whom needed treatment in the emergency room.

Despite the violence and near chaos, the procession continued to its end at the steps of the US Treasury Building. There, suffragists dressed in flowing robes and colorful scarves staged an elaborate pageant to show "those ideals toward which both men and women have been struggling through the ages and toward which, in cooperation and equality, they will continue to strive." The *New York Times* called it "one of the most impressively beautiful spectacles ever staged in this country."

KNOW YOUR RADICALS:
ᴔ IDA B. WELLS ᴕ

African American women were active participants and leaders of the suffrage movement despite facing discrimination from many white suffragists. They were driven by a belief that the vote could be used to improve their status as both female *and* African American. Like their white counterparts, they tended to be well educated and relatively wealthy, such as the influential Mary Church Terrell, who was an effective national leader for both suffrage and civil rights. The importance of race for African American suffragists grew over time. Frances Harper, another leading African American suffragist, put it this way: "As much as white women need the ballot, colored women need it more."

Perhaps the most remarkable female African American

A young Ida B. Wells, late nineteenth century.

suffragist was Ida B. Wells. Wells was born in Mississippi in 1862. Her parents both died from yellow fever in 1878, leaving sixteen-year-old Ida responsible for her six siblings, so she took a teaching job to support everyone.

Less than ten years later, Wells began her lifelong project of challenging the place of African Americans in society. In 1884 she sat in the ladies' section of a train rather than in the "colored" section. When a conductor ordered her to move, she refused. When he attempted to move her by force, she bit his hand before being dragged off the train. Later Wells hired a lawyer and sued the railroad. She won a five-hundred-dollar judgment, though a higher court would eventually reverse the ruling.

As she grew older, Wells came to recognize the importance of media and defiant journalism. She contributed to and even co-owned newspapers. Starting in the 1890s, she began a campaign to draw attention to the horrific practice of lynching, which typically involved southern whites taking the law into their own hands by hanging African Americans. Wells systematically uncovered the terrifying frequency of lynching and debunked the widely accepted but baseless theory that lynchings were always a direct response to sexual attacks by African American men on white women. She exposed the fact that African Americans were often lynched for minor or nonexistent offenses, such as not repaying a debt. In doing so, Wells showed that the real cause of lynching was murderous racism itself. Her investigative journalism changed the way many Americans understood this appalling problem.

Wells eventually moved to Chicago, where she founded the Alpha Suffrage Club in 1913, the same year that Illinois became the first state east of the Mississippi to grant women the right to vote. The Alpha Suffrage Club would become the most important African American suffrage organization in the country. Wells and her club quickly began organizing, with an eye toward influencing local Chicago politics. In 1915 they scored a major success, helping Oscar De Priest become Chicago's first African American alderman. Wells's club demonstrated the power African American women could wield when they organized behind a political cause.

The parade was a huge success, and the violent crowds and police inaction only multiplied the intense publicity. The national press was up in arms about the terrible way the marchers had been treated, and its response had a meaningful impact on public opinion. Congressional hearings were held to investigate the police, and the testimony lasted for two weeks, as 150 people recounted their experiences. In the end, the Washington, D.C., chief of police lost his job. Suffrage returned to the front pages of the nation's newspapers and received highly sympathetic coverage.

Officially, Alice Paul was still just the twenty-eight-year-old chair of the NAWSA's marginal Congressional Committee. But in three short months—with the help of Lucy Burns and thousands of others—she had succeeded in jump-starting a stalled movement. Without a doubt the fight for suffrage was back on track. And Paul was only warming up. Following the parade, she fixed her eyes on her ultimate target: Woodrow Wilson, the newly inaugurated president of the United States.

PUTTING IT IN PERSPECTIVE:
ഏ SUFFRAGE IN THE WEST ൭

Why was it that the first four states to give women the right to vote were Wyoming, Utah, Colorado, and Idaho? And why did both Wyoming and Utah, still just territories back then, enfranchise women less than five years after the end of the Civil War—that is, a full half century before women got the right to vote nationwide?

The men in these states were not unusually liberal and progressive. No, women's suffrage was supported in these states for a variety of practical political reasons.

First, men outnumbered women by significant margins in these sparsely inhabited territories. This presented a problem when it came to starting families and building permanent communities. Many believed that extending suffrage to women would attract new female settlers to the region.

Second, many of those supporting suffrage believed it was a good way to publicize their territories. By calling for suffrage, they could attract new residents and thus new opportunities for business and investors. Advocates didn't fear the political power suffrage would give women since they were so outnumbered by men.

Moreover, because western cities and towns were relatively new, women in places like Wyoming tended to be less politically organized than those in more established communities back east, and thus they posed little threat to the current political order.

Third, because of the overall small populations in places like Wyoming and Utah, many easterners felt safe supporting and funding suffrage campaigns for women in the West in order to see what would actually happen when women started voting. The results, if negative, would have no direct effect on their states back east. And since the numbers in the West were dwarfed by those in the East, it was highly unlikely that these newly enfranchised women could make a meaningful impact on national politics.

All in all, the West's support of women's suffrage had little to do with what was right. Nevertheless, these states helped the rest of the nation see that women could vote without negative consequences. Progress is progress, even when its supporters aren't all that progressive.

This cartoon appeared in Puck *magazine on February 20, 1915, and shows Lady Liberty striding across the country toward states that had yet to adopt women's suffrage.*

CHAPTER

The Long Showdown and a Night of Terror

As Alice Paul and Lucy Burns gradually took control of the push for suffrage, they would make the movement more confrontational and less willing to compromise than ever before. Their demands would be met with resistance, some of it quite violent. After enduring a final, horrible escalation in 1917, these brave, determined activists finally reached the doorstep of success.

The parade on March 2 was a major achievement. A normal leader might have taken some time off in order to relax and enjoy the victory. Indeed, Lucy Burns did just that, returning home for a few weeks to visit family. But Alice Paul was no normal leader. While the congressional hearings to investigate police conduct during the parade were still underway, Paul decided to organize a group of suffragists to meet with the new president. Such a meeting was simply easier to arrange back then: the president was much more accessible to the public, and it didn't hurt that

Paul's group included women related to congressmen or married to people of influence in Washington.

On March 17, Paul led a group of women into the White House. President Wilson had arranged five chairs in a semicircle for his guests. He sat in another chair facing them. Wilson, a one-time professor, expected that this brief gathering (he agreed to give them only ten minutes of his time) would unfold much like a meeting between a teacher and his obedient students. But even though the fifty-seven-year-old president was twice Paul's age, it was he who was about to learn a thing or two.

Paul stated that suffrage was "the paramount"—that is, most important—"issue of the day." The president listened politely and then told the women that he had no opinion on the subject. His main responsibility, he claimed, was getting Congress to focus on the crucial economic issues of the day: currency revision and tariff reform. Wilson probably assumed that the women would then smile and leave, grateful for the opportunity to have met with him. Instead Paul responded, "But Mr. President, do you not understand that the Administration has no right to legislate for currency, tariff, and any other reform without first getting the consent of women?"

With this bold question, Paul made it clear why she believed her cause to be paramount. If half the population had no say in elections, the American government was illegitimate. In Alice Paul's eyes the situation was as simple as that. And by stating the matter so directly, Paul also made it clear that she wasn't intimidated by anyone, not even the president of the United States. In the years to come, Wilson would learn this again and again.

But for now he merely answered, "This subject will receive my most careful consideration." And with that the meeting was over.

Wilson was not entirely honest during this conversation. He did, in fact, have an opinion on suffrage for women: he was opposed to it. In general, the president viewed women as very different from men. He didn't believe that women thought or made decisions like men, and for this reason he concluded that women could not understand politics. And someone who doesn't understand politics most certainly shouldn't vote.

Alice Paul may or may not have known this about Wilson. Regardless, it wouldn't have influenced her actions. She believed that the president was the key to getting a national amendment, so he had to be pressured constantly. With this in mind, Paul sent two more groups to the White House over the next few weeks. Determined to build on their momentum and attention in the press, Paul and Burns organized another mass demonstration for April 7, 1913, which also happened to be Congress' first day in session during Wilson's presidency.

Paul wanted the president to know that his promise of "careful consideration" would not satisfy her for long.

———◦◈◦———

In just a few months, Alice Paul and Lucy Burns had quickly emerged as a dynamic force in the suffrage movement, injecting it with new life. Naturally, many of their fellow activists were excited by this development. But not everyone was pleased, including the long-standing leadership of the movement itself.

In 1913, Anna Howard Shaw stood at the head of the NAWSA. Despite stepping down from this position eight years before, Carrie Chapman Catt was still very involved and would return as president of the organization in 1915. At first Shaw and Catt were thrilled by the younger pair's energy and resourcefulness. Immediately after the parade, Shaw wrote to Paul that "the National Association will never cease to be grateful to you all for the splendid service you have done in its name." But within a few short months the older leadership would come to view Burns and especially Paul as threats to their control over the movement. Paul's Congressional Committee was an official arm of the NAWSA, but now it was taking on a life of its own— as well as taking funds, members, and attention away from the NAWSA itself.

More than this, Paul's tactics and goals clashed with the NAWSA's. The NAWSA dealt with politicians in an agreeable, "ladylike" fashion. In addition to Catt's preference for compromise, Shaw was strongly opposed to militancy of any kind. And of course, the NAWSA had long since settled on a state-by-state strategy, whereas Paul was interested only in a national amendment. The NAWSA had seen some recent victories, as Washington, California, Arizona, Kansas, and Oregon had given women the vote by 1913. Nevertheless, in April of that year Paul formed the Congressional Union (CU), an organization dedicated exclusively to getting a national amendment. The CU was part of the NAWSA, but operated with more freedom than the Congressional Committee did.

Before the next year was out, though, an additional disagreement would lead to Paul and Burns splitting off from the NAWSA altogether. For years the NAWSA had been "nonpartisan," meaning the organization refused to side with either the Republican or Democratic party, choosing instead to work with (or patiently wait for the help of) leaders from both parties. Paul thought this was foolish, because in 1913 the Democratic Party was incredibly powerful. Not only was President Wilson a Democrat, but the Democrats controlled Congress as well.

Paul came to a simple conclusion: if one party has all the power and is dragging its feet on the matter of women's suffrage, this party must be opposed. In the 1914 elections, the CU openly campaigned against all Democratic candidates in the nine states where women could already vote. Paul explained the reason for this: "Not because we do not like the Democrats, but because the Democratic party has proved so effectively that it dislikes us." Shaw and Catt strongly opposed this new strategy, labeling it "militant" and "un-American." The CU's strategy proved somewhat successful, but another split in the suffrage movement was now underway.

———◦◖◗◦———

By 1916 the CU had considerable momentum. Since the time of its formation, both the Senate and House had actually voted on— but not approved—a federal amendment for women's suffrage. The president, under constant pressure, was gradually shifting his public excuse from not knowing "what his position might be on this new matter" to "I am not at liberty until I speak for somebody besides myself to urge legislation upon the Congress" to a belief that "suffrage ought to be brought about state by state." Indeed, Wilson himself had voted for the New Jersey state suffrage referendum in 1915 (though he knew it would lose).

Meanwhile, Burns and especially Paul worked day and night to keep the issue in the public eye, thereby forcing politicians to address it. Parades and demonstrations became regular happenings across the nation, as did deputations and other forms of lobbying in Washington, D.C. A highly publicized cross-country car trip by two activists transported a massive, eighteen-thousand-foot-long petition with more than five hundred thousand signatures from San Francisco to the nation's capital. The CU even moved into new headquarters right by the White House to demonstrate that this organization was not to be ignored.

Despite all this, Alice Paul and Lucy Burns were far from satisfied. Though they had only been working for a fraction of the time that Elizabeth Cady Stanton, Susan B. Anthony, and so many others before them had spent laboring for suffrage, they were much less patient. When they had first returned from Europe, Paul and Burns naively believed that a federal amendment could be obtained within a year. Now a few years had come and gone, and neither was willing to dig in for a decades-long struggle. So with the 1916 elections approaching, they decided to form a new political party, one solely devoted to getting a national amendment.

The Woman's Party convention was held in Chicago on June 5, 1916. This party, soon to be renamed the National Woman's Party (NWP), marked the first time in American history that voting women organized themselves within the party system. In stark contrast to most political parties, the NWP did not promote candidates of its own. Instead the NWP advanced a single-issue platform: the immediate passage of a federal suffrage amendment. If the party in power—in this case the Democrats—did not clearly and officially support such an amendment, the NWP would mobilize women who already had the vote (in states like

Wyoming and Colorado) to vote against its candidates.

This new party quickly affected the political climate. Even before the 1916 election, both the Democrats and the Republicans, for the first time ever, acknowledged the importance of women's suffrage in their platforms. The Republican nominee for president, Charles Evans Hughes, went even further and endorsed the so-called Anthony Amendment, a first for a major-party candidate for president.

But Woodrow Wilson, up for reelection as the Democratic nominee, did not. Europe was being torn apart by World War I, and Wilson had succeeded so far in keeping the United States out of the conflict. Wilson campaigned with the slogan "He kept us out of war." Many people supported him for this, but Paul and the NWP responded with a slogan of their own: "He kept us out of suffrage." The NWP did not officially endorse Hughes and the Republicans, but rather campaigned *against* Wilson and the Democrats.

Despite the opposition of the NWP, Wilson won a second term in 1916. Nevertheless, the NWP had reason to be optimistic. In those states where women could vote, he won fewer votes than he had in 1912. And in the one state, Illinois, where women's votes were tallied separately, Hughes beat Wilson among female voters by a ratio of two to one.

But again Alice Paul was far from satisfied.

————◦◎◦————

The arduous 1916 election campaign was over, but Paul wasn't about to take a rest. Her next step came in response to a horrible tragedy within the suffrage movement.

Inez Milholland (center) stands with two other women at the National Woman's Party headquarters in Washington, D.C., 1916.

Inez Milholland, the woman in white who led the March 3, 1913, parade, had been sent out west to campaign for the NWP during the 1916 elections. Traveling with her sister, she planned to appear in more than thirty cities in a month's time. This demanding tour took a lot out of her, something not helped by the fact that she was ill even before it began. Battling infections and an "erratic heart," Milholland tried to keep up with the schedule, which only made her condition worse. In late November, a few weeks after the election, Milholland died. She was only thirty years old.

Milholland was immediately transformed into a martyr for the cause—that is, a woman who had sacrificed herself for suffrage. On Christmas Day a memorial pageant was held for her in Washington, D.C.'s National Statuary Hall in the US Capitol Building, a grand structure housing statues of former presidents and other American leaders. Another memorial took place in early January, when three hundred women marched from CU headquarters to the White House. There they eulogized Milholland to the president, and asked him to support the amendment in order to prevent further sacrifice. But Wilson merely responded, "It is impossible for me, until the orders of my party are changed, to do anything other than what I am doing as a party leader." He turned and left.

The women returned to headquarters, outraged by the president's ridiculous excuse. Executive power (that is, the power of the president) may have been weaker in 1917 than it is today, but Wilson certainly could have chosen to support suffrage publicly as president. A meeting was held. Harriot Stanton Blatch, one of Elizabeth Cady Stanton's daughters and a leader in the movement, inspired her fellow activists. "We have got to take a new departure," she said, recognizing that their current strategies were not effective enough. She continued, "We have got to bring to the President, individually, day by day, week in and week out, the idea that great numbers of women want to be free, will be free, and want to know what he is going to do about it."

Blatch suggested a new tactic: "Let us stand beside the gateway where he must pass in and out, so that he can never fail to realize that there is a tremendous earnestness and insistence back of this measure." It was decided: the women would picket the White House. Blatch had proposed the idea, but as usual Paul would oversee its execution.

On January 10, 1917, at ten in the morning, twelve women assembled around the gates of the White House, through which the president would come and go. They wore sashes of purple, white, and gold—the colors of the suffrage movement—and held high large banners that read, "Mr. President What Will You Do for Woman Suffrage" and "Mr. President How Long Must Women Wait for Liberty." That morning the president passed by them on his way back from a golf game. He pretended they weren't there.

These women were the first people in American history to picket the White House. This crucial tactic was a perfect example of the way Alice Paul applied what she had learned from the Pankhursts without just borrowing from them blindly. Though she was often called "militant," this was not an accurate label for Paul and her wing of the movement. She chose tactics that were confrontational but still nonviolent. As we'll see, the picketers—or "Silent Sentinels," as they came to be called— would soon engage in the kind of civil disobedience that Martin Luther King Jr. and the civil rights movement would make famous decades later.

Women picketing the White House, February 1917.

Women picketed the White House from ten in the morning until five in the evening, six days a week, no matter the weather, for many, many months. The Sentinels received considerable publicity and also became a tourist attraction. For a while Wilson seemed mostly amused by them, assuming they would give up soon enough. As he passed them each day he would nod, smile, wave, and tip his hat. On one cold, snowy day, he even had them invited inside, but they refused. They didn't want his hospitality; they wanted his power behind their cause.

On April 6, 1917, the United States officially entered World War I. There was enormous pressure throughout the country for everyone, including suffragists, to drop their differences and get behind the war effort. The NAWSA agreed to suspend suffrage activity until the conflict was over.

But Alice Paul and her followers did not. The president argued that America must enter the war to make the world "safe for democracy." Because democracy in the United States was still incomplete, Paul viewed Wilson's statement as hypocrisy. She put it like this: "It will always be difficult to wage a war for democracy abroad while democracy is denied at home." So the picketing continued, while the language of the banners changed to draw attention to the flaw in Wilson's argument for going to war. One now read, "Democracy must begin at Home."

On June 20, Paul chose to escalate the confrontation between the NWP and the president. That day a delegation of America's Russian allies visited the White House. A special message—written on an extra-large banner, just for them—greeted their car as it passed through the gates: "President Wilson and Envoy Root are deceiving Russia. We women of America tell you that America is not a democracy. Twenty million American women are denied the right to vote. President Wilson is the chief opponent of their national enfranchisement. Help us make our government really free. Tell our government that it must liberate its people before it can claim free Russia as an ally."

All along, the purpose of the Silent Sentinels had been to embarrass the president. That day they finally succeeded. Before this Wilson had instructed the police and his own Secret Service not to interfere with the protests. But soon after the Russian visit, the chief of police informed Paul that future picketers would be arrested. "We have picketed for six months without interference," she told him. *"Has the law been changed? . . .* We have consulted our lawyers and know we have a legal right to picket." The chief of police merely repeated his warning.

On June 22, the first arrests took place. The charge? Obstructing traffic. The women's cases were dropped. But when the picketing continued, four more arrests were made. These women were tried and sentenced to pay a twenty-five-dollar fine or serve three days in jail. Echoing Susan B. Anthony's words from nearly half a century earlier, the women spoke defiantly: "Not a dollar of your fine shall we pay. To pay a fine would be an admission of guilt. We are innocent." So they went to jail.

The showdown intensified. On July 14, sixteen Sentinels were arrested. They used their trial to make their case to the public: "We know full well that we stand here because the President of the United States refuses to give liberty to American women." But the judge was not convinced. The women were sentenced to sixty days, this time in the dreaded Occoquan Workhouse in Virginia. Entering Occoquan was like walking into a nightmare. The cells, small and dark, were rat-infested. The very best food there was dirty, sour soup, because the solid food was riddled with worms.

But after three days, thanks to direct pressure on the president from near and far, the women were pardoned and released. Lucy Burns came to the prison to help the women travel back to Washington, D.C. The head of Occoquan, superintendent Raymond Whittaker, addressed her: "Now that you women are going away, I have something to say to *you.* The next lot of women who come here won't be treated with the same consideration that these women were."

—•—◦⊗◦—•—

Alice Paul understood perfectly well that the greatest powers women without the vote possessed were the attention of the press and the sympathy of the nation. These two forces placed pressure on the politicians. But attention is hard to keep, and sympathy easily fades. Because of this, Paul regularly sought to intensify the clash with Wilson. For example, the Silent Sentinels constantly changed the words on their banners, often to make their messages more confrontational.

On August 14, such confrontation reached a new level with a banner that referred to the president as "Kaiser," which was the title of the enemy German leader. This was viewed by many as treasonous. The women didn't just lose some sympathy for their decision; they were physically attacked by their fellow citizens, many of them soldiers and sailors in uniform.

The picketers' "Kaiser" banners were torn apart at the White House gates. Replacement banners were brought over, but these were destroyed as well. Eventually the mob, ignored by the police, attacked the NWP

Suffragist Virginia Arnold poses with a Kaiser Wilson banner, August 14, 1917.

headquarters. A sailor punched a young suffragist in the face. Lucy Burns was nearly tossed over a balcony railing. Police only stopped the riot when a bullet came through a window, lodging in the ceiling.

The violence continued in the days to come. More banners were destroyed, and Alice Paul was knocked down and dragged along the sidewalk. Fifty policemen actually joined the mob on August 16 as the attacks escalated. Still, the women would not back down. So the arrests began again, and women were sent back to Occoquan, this time for longer.

Paul and the rest of the women had a decision to make: should they suspend picketing and soften their message in order to win back sympathy, or continue their showdown with the authorities? Paul chose confrontation, gambling that harsher punishment would put the pressure back on President Wilson. This time she would seek imprisonment herself, knowing her suffering would draw attention to the government's treatment of women as a whole.

In October, along with other activists, Paul picketed numerous times and was repeatedly arrested. On October 20, she held a banner that read, "The time has come to conquer or submit. For us there can be but one choice," and was arrested once more. This time she was sentenced to seven months in prison. The longest sentence a suffragist had previously received was sixty days.

Paul began a hunger strike and was soon force-fed three times a day. She demanded political prisoner status from both the courts and the prison, which would have required her arrest to be viewed as a protest against an unfair government rather than a criminal act. Instead of meeting her demand, the authorities separated Paul from the rest of the prisoners in the District Jail and placed her in a psychiatric ward. Not even her lawyer could visit her.

Paul now confronted a new danger. If a doctor diagnosed her as mentally ill, she could be moved to an insane asylum and kept there indefinitely. In an effort to weaken her mental state, the door to her room was removed and the windows boarded up. A guard woke her every hour with a bright light, which led to sleep deprivation, a classic torture technique. Meanwhile, a doctor questioned her each day, hoping to hear that she viewed Wilson as a personal enemy. That would have been enough to declare her insane and have her taken away.

Alice Paul, physically frail to begin with, was weakened further by her hunger strike and lack of sleep. But thanks to her extraordinary mental toughness she never broke. Nevertheless, the experience was terrifying. Years later she would recall, "I believe I have never in my life before feared anything or any human being. But I confess I was afraid of Dr. Gannon. . . . I dreaded the hour of his visit."

With Paul in jail, the other activists continued picketing, and arrests piled up at an incredible rate. Seventy women were arrested in October alone. In mid-November thirty-five women were arrested, and many of them, including Lucy Burns, received six-month-long sentences.

Rather than taking them to the District Jail where Paul was being held, the authorities returned them to Occoquan. Here Superintendent Whittaker finally acted on the threat he had made to Burns back in July. He burst into the holding room where the women were waiting, accompanied by up to forty club-wielding men, some of whom were not even in uniform. Whittaker began shouting out orders to his men, and women were soon being dragged violently to cells and tossed inside. Dorothy Day was slammed down twice over the back of an iron bench. Dora Lewis was thrown into her cell with such force she was knocked unconscious. Alice M. Cosu suffered a heart attack, and her calls for help were ignored all night long.

Women were beaten, kicked, and choked. The superintendent viewed Lucy Burns, recently freed after serving a sixty-day sentence, as the ringleader. She was taken to her cell, where her hands were cuffed and fastened to the cell door above her head. Her clothes were stripped, and she was left with only a blanket. Despite this, she called out to the other women throughout the night, even after being threatened with a gag and straitjacket.

Suffragist Kate Heffelfinger is escorted out of Occoquan Workhouse, circa 1917. She was jailed many times for picketing.

This night, which has come to be known as the "Night of Terror" in the history of women's suffrage in America, marked the climax of the decades-long showdown between female activists and male authorities. In their effort to win a say in how they would be governed, these women—along with Alice Paul, who spent this night enduring her own form of "administrative terrorism" in a psychiatric ward—were brutalized by their government.

Despite all they went through that night, the women began a hunger strike the next day. Soon details of their imprisonment began to reach the press. The judge presiding over a November 23 hearing about the situation of the women at Occoquan was alarmed by the sight of them and their descriptions of their treatment. President Wilson, who publicly had ignored the situation, was finally forced to take action. David Lawrence, a journalist and close friend of the president, soon visited Paul in jail, where a negotiation began. What, he asked, would convince the women to stop their picketing? "Nothing short of the passage of the amendment through Congress will end our agitation," she told him. Lawrence told her the president would encourage congressmen to support the amendment the next time it came up for a vote.

On November 27 and 28 all the suffrage prisoners were suddenly released. A terribly frail Paul, who had been on hunger strike for twenty-two days, spoke to the press: "We are put out of jail as we were put in—at the whim of the government. They tried to terrorize and suppress us. They could not, so they freed us."

AROUND THE WORLD:
WHEN DID WOMEN WIN THE RIGHT ∾ TO VOTE IN OTHER COUNTRIES? ∾

Considering the fact that it took American women more than seventy years to gain the right to vote, it seems like their victory must have come awfully late. But did it? Relative to other countries throughout the world, when did American women win this right? Were they among the first? The last?

The first country to grant women the right to vote was Sweden, way back in 1718. But the right was conditional, constantly chang-ing, and eventually revoked altogether in 1772. Swedish women wouldn't have the right to vote in national elections until 1919, and wouldn't actually have an election to vote in until 1921. So perhaps it's wrong to say Sweden was first.

The first place to permanently grant women the right to vote was New Zealand in 1893, when it wasn't yet an independent country (it would become independent in 1907). A year later, in 1894, the colony of South Australia followed suit. And unlike New Zealand, Australia granted women the right to do more than just vote; they could run for government positions as well.

Finland was next in 1906. It also became the first country to elect women to its parliament. Another eight countries—Norway, Denmark, Canada, Austria, Germany, Poland, Russia, and the Netherlands—would also have women voters before the United States, leaving the US in thirteenth place overall, though it should be noted that in Canada and Australia, native peoples of both sexes (First Nations people in Canada and Aborigines in Austra-lia) weren't allowed to vote until 1960 and 1962, respectively.

So the United States was definitely not the first, but it was much, much closer to first than last. More than a hundred nations achieved universal suffrage after the US.

And which country was last? That dubious distinction goes to Saudi Arabia, where women were given the right to vote in mu-nicipal elections only in 2011. Women actually voted for the first time—and were allowed to run for office—in 2015. Sometimes history is barely in the past at all.

CHAPTER

War of the Roses: The Final Battle for the Right to Vote

Even after President Wilson offered his clear support for the Susan B. Anthony Amendment, additional hurdles still remained. Both houses of Congress needed to approve the amendment. If and when that happened, three out of every four state legislatures would have to do the same. Almost two more years of hard work would be needed before an unlikely drama unfolded in Tennessee's state legislature and made history.

On December 3, 1917, just a week after the suffrage prisoners had been freed from the Occoquan Workhouse, the House of Representatives declared it would vote on the Nineteenth Amendment, which would grant women the right to vote, the following month. But President Wilson addressed Congress on that same December day and made no mention of suffrage. Instead he focused on his fourteen-point peace plan for ending World War I. Would he ever publicly get behind the amendment?

The answer came on January 9, 1918, the day before the pivotal vote on the amendment, when a delegation of Democratic representatives visited the White House. Many of these elected officials were unsure of how to vote and sought guidance from the leader of their party. The president encouraged them to support the amendment, and a public statement was released. It read:

> *The President had not felt at liberty to volunteer his advice to members of congress on this important matter; but when we sought his advice he very frankly and earnestly advised us to vote for the amendment . . . as an act of right and justice to the women of the country and of the world.*

The next day, January 10, the House of Representatives debated the amendment for hours. The supporters' determination to get it passed was unmistakable. One elderly representative showed up despite a broken shoulder. Two more arrived straight from their hospital beds. Another came to vote even though his wife, a longtime supporter of suffrage, had passed away the night before. When the vote was finally taken, 274 were in favor and 136 were opposed. Forty years to the day after the amendment was first brought before Congress, it passed, with precisely the two-thirds majority required.

A celebration erupted throughout the House of Representatives. Suffragists who had followed the debate from the gallery hugged one another and wept with relief. The women broke out in song and marched victoriously back to headquarters to inform Alice Paul, who had left the House that afternoon, likely because she was certain of the outcome. They found their leader, who would turn thirty-two the next day, bent over her desk, busy as always. Her response to the wonderful, historic news? "Eleven to win before we can pass the Senate."

Paul believed they were still eleven votes short of passing the amendment in the Senate, where it would go next. She saw no reason for celebration; it was time to get back to work.

The next phase of the activists' campaign involved lobbying senators constantly, both in Washington and back in their home states. Intense research was done to identify any senator who might be willing to switch from opposing the amendment to supporting it. Who were the people in his life who held the greatest influence over him? Was his wife or mother a supporter of suffrage? Paul kept meticulous notes on every senator, determined to find an opening or a weakness that could get her a vote.

By May, nine senators were won over to suffrage's side. But then opposition senators used the filibuster—in which they extended debate on the amendment indefinitely—to prevent the scheduled June 27 vote from even taking place. In July the Senate took a recess and would not reconvene until the fall. The momentum from the successful House of Representatives vote was long gone.

What would the suffragists' next step be? Alice Paul explained it in a newspaper interview: "Whenever we picketed the White House, we noticed the president became more active in our cause, and whenever we let up there was a relaxation." It was true: back in January President Wilson had encouraged House members to vote for the amendment, but since that time he had been quiet on the matter. Surely he could exert more pressure on his fellow Democrats in the Senate, but this would require more pressure on the president.

So the picketing began again. As did the arrests. In August, twenty-six women, instead of being sent to a regular jail, were imprisoned in a building that had been condemned a decade earlier. There the prisoners fell ill from water tainted by the building's rusty pipes, so ill that many of them could hardly walk to the ambulances waiting for them upon their release five days later.

Again their suffering led to renewed, vocal support for their cause. A number of leading senators visited the imprisoned women and complained to the administration. For the first time, the minority Republican Party called for a vote in the Senate, but the cooperation of Democratic senators was necessary for the amendment to come to the floor.

In order to keep pressure on those dragging their feet, Paul chose September 16 for the next mass demonstration. Earlier that same day Wilson met with a delegation of Democratic women not affiliated with Paul's organization and declared that he was "heartily in sympathy" with the suffrage cause. Perhaps this was true, but if he really meant it, why wasn't he working harder to persuade Democrats in the Senate—especially when they had just announced they had no intention of voting on the Nineteenth Amendment in the near future?

The protesters decided that Wilson's words were empty and responded by taking a new, bold step. A torch had been brought to this protest to symbolize "the burning indignation of women who for a hundred years have been given words without action." But the demonstrators soon found another use for it: they took the words the president had spoken to the women earlier that day—"I shall do all that I can"—and burned them on the spot. This action was met with applause, and no one was arrested.

The next day the Senate suffrage committee placed the Anthony Amendment on the Senate calendar.

The vote was scheduled for September 26, 1918. President Wilson arrived in the Senate chambers that day and spoke emotionally in support of the amendment. "It is my duty," he said, "to win the war and to ask you to remove every obstacle that stands in the way of winning it." Finally the president was arguing that patriotism and suffrage were connected. Many people assumed that the president's speech would convince those Senators on the fence to get behind the amendment. But his words were not enough, and the measure lost by two votes.

————◦◉◦————

Dealt another defeat, Paul and the NWP turned their attention to the November elections, which were fast approaching. Thanks to the ongoing efforts of the NAWSA, there were more states than ever before, including New York, where women could vote. The NWP was determined to take advantage of the NAWSA's successes by punishing Senate Democrats for failing to support suffrage. And punished they would be. The Republicans picked up six Senate seats in the elections. Wilson would be working with a Republican-controlled Congress for the first time in his presidency.

President Wilson opened the next congressional session on December 2, and mentioned suffrage, but would he do anything more about it? Thanks to the elections, the numbers in the Senate were now favorable for a vote, but getting that vote to take place was another matter altogether. Anti-suffrage Senators were now working behind the scenes to keep another vote off the calendar.

If the Senate didn't vote on the amendment before it adjourned for the year in early March, the entire process—beginning with the House of Representatives—would need to start all over again.

Wilson's public plea to Congress wasn't enough. And ten days later he sailed to France to work on the peace agreements following the end of World War I, which had finally concluded the previous month. Wilson had an elaborate vision for a so-called "League of Nations," which he hoped would prevent the kind of horrible conflict that cost ten million lives across Europe. In truth, suffrage was still not a priority for him.

In Europe Wilson would meet with leaders of Russia and England—countries where women could vote—to discuss the fate of Germany, where women could vote as well. In response, suffragists held another mass demonstration on December 16. Fifty women bearing torches marched into Lafayette Park, just a few hundred feet from the White House. A large Grecian urn was placed on the ground, and a fire was lit inside it. Woman after woman tossed a different speech given by the absent president into the urn, where it burned. The president, these women argued, spoke often about liberty and democracy, but failed to make it a reality at home.

On New Year's Day, 1919, to mark the year Paul called "Victory New Year," the urn was moved to the sidewalk outside the White House. Wood from Independence Square in Philadelphia, where the US Constitution was first ratified, was brought in to keep the urn's fire lit indefinitely. Meanwhile, a bell was hung from the balcony of the nearby NWP headquarters. Each time it rang, different words from the president were tossed into the fire. For a few days police allowed the suffragists to guard the fire around the clock. But soon the charges of obstructing traffic, and the arrests, began again. Once more a new tactic had led to another showdown, all of which brought renewed publicity to the cause and heightened pressure on Wilson to act.

The president, still in Europe, started cabling Democrats in the Senate to schedule a vote. The date was finally set for February 10. Despite this achievement, Paul and her supporters decided to show their contempt toward Wilson for not acting sooner and more aggressively. On February 9, suffragists burned him in effigy outside of the White House. Many arrests resulted from what is widely seen as Paul's least popular act of public protest.

The following day the vote lost again, this time by only one vote. Even Carrie Chapman Catt, now head of the nonpartisan NAWSA, conceded that the Democrats were to blame. Their "no" votes outnumbered Republican "no" votes by almost two to one. Congress would adjourn without passing the Nineteenth Amendment.

Still, the suffragists now knew that the tide was turning in support of suffrage. Thanks to the steady, if often unsuccessful, state-by-state strategy of the NAWSA, a majority of states had some form of suffrage for women. Victories for women's suffrage had been won in Scandinavia and England. The new Republican-led Congress would soon demonstrate American support for enfranchising women. Nevertheless, the suffragists kept up their protests and clashes with the police until Wilson, still in Europe, called a special session of Congress to vote on the Anthony Amendment on May 19, 1919.

Both the House of Representatives and the Senate had to vote, and the numbers in this new Congress were very different.

On May 21, the House passed the Nineteenth Amendment overwhelmingly, 304–89. Two weeks later, on June 4, the Senate voted
56–25 to do the same. Unlike when the House had passed the
amendment the first time, celebrations were muted, perhaps because suffragists were long since fed up with the painfully slow
process. As one activist, Maud Younger, would write in her memoir, "There was no excitement. . . . A whole year had passed in
the winning of two votes. Everyone knew what the end would be
now. It was all very dull."

Plus, the amendment wasn't yet law. One last hurdle remained: state ratification.

————◦◈◦————

By the time of the Senate vote, twenty-eight out of the forty-eight
states that then made up the United States had approved some
form of women's suffrage. That was eight states short of the three-
fourths majority needed to ratify the amendment. In addition,
only fifteen of those twenty-eight states had approved unlimited
suffrage for women. The other thirteen restricted which elections
women could vote in. Worse yet, voting rights for women within
a particular state did not guarantee that its legislature would
support a national amendment.

Still, signs were hopeful at first, as eleven states rushed to ratify the amendment within a month. That was almost one-third of
what was needed. But getting another twenty-five states to ratify
wouldn't be easy.

The next wave of states to ratify did so thanks in large part
to Carrie Chapman Catt and the NAWSA. Paul may have made
more progress in seven years than Catt had made in twenty,

Colorado Governor Oliver Henry Shoup signs his state's ratification of the suffrage amendment, December 12, 1919.

but Catt's experience working with states made her a priceless asset when it came to navigating local politics. Her vast lobbying network fought tirelessly to push governors to call special sessions in many states to vote on the amendment. By February 1920, thirty-two states had ratified suffrage. Only four more to go.

As summer neared, three more states ratified the amendment. But there were few likely candidates to become the thirty-sixth and final state to climb on board. Ratification seemed stuck, and if another state didn't join the majority it was a distinct possibility that many women would be unable to vote in the presidential election later that year.

But in mid-June, thanks to its governor, a special session of the Tennessee legislature was called. Just like that, all eyes turned to the Volunteer State.

Suffragists worried about the likelihood of Tennessee's support, since it was located in the South, where opposition to women's suffrage was strongest. Why were many in the South against giving women the right to vote? First, they viewed the passage of any federal amendment as a threat to states' rights, something highly valued in the South since at least the time of the Civil War. Second, residents of these states tended to hold more traditional views of women and their place in society. Women voting, many believed, would weaken marriages and even destroy the home. Last, giving women the vote officially meant giving African American women the vote as well. Much of the American South still held racist views and resented the passage of the Fourteenth Amendment, which gave African American men the vote, half a century earlier.

The good news was that, despite all of this, in 1919 Tennessee had passed a law giving women the right to vote in presidential and city elections. In addition, the state Democratic Party, its governor, and most of the state's newspapers supported suffrage. That's why supporters of suffrage chose to concentrate their resources and efforts in Tennessee and not in North Carolina, where a ratification vote was also scheduled. When it came to Tennessee, there was reason to be confident and reason to fear defeat. In fact, the only clear thing about the upcoming vote in the Volunteer State was that it was going to be close and bitterly fought.

And so Carrie Chapman Catt took a train to Nashville, Tennessee, on July 17. She came with just a single small bag, planning to stick around for only a few days to help get the pro-suffrage campaign off the ground. She would remain in Tennessee for more than a month, enduring stifling heat and fighting the opposition in its many forms. The cause for suffrage might have been lofty, but the battle she faced was not. In fact, it was flat-out nasty. As she put it, "Ratification in Tennessee will go through the work and actions of men, and the great motive that will finally put it through will be political and nothing else. We have long since recovered from our previous faith in the action of men based upon a love of justice. That is an animal that doesn't exist."

Alice Paul chose not to go to Nashville, in part because the more radical NWP was strongly disliked in much of the state. Her presence might have served only to energize the opposition. All the same, she sent numerous representatives to work for the cause. Since 1913 Paul had been the leader in the long march for suffrage, but she now passed the baton back to Catt for the last lap. Catt toured the state relentlessly, coordinated suffrage activity, and urged the various NAWSA and NWP activists to put aside differences and fight together for a common cause.

———◦◈◦———

The seventy-year-long battle for women's suffrage had come down not just to a single state but, in fact, to a single hotel. The Hermitage, located in Nashville just down the hill from the State Capitol, hosted not only Catt but also Josephine Anderson Pearson, the president of the Tennessee State Association Opposed to Woman Suffrage.

Governor Roberts had called for the special session to open on August 9, and soon many legislators began arriving at the Hermitage, too. They quickly found themselves thrust into the "War of the Roses," as the newspapers soon called it. Those opposed to suffrage wore red roses; those for it wore yellow. Soon every man in the hotel had a rose on his lapel. It was impossible

An anti-suffrage songbook featuring the red rose that represented the anti-suffrage movement, 1915.

to remain neutral in such an environment. The Hermitage was no longer a hotel; it was a battlefield.

The opposition camp included not just individuals, but also giant business interests like the alcohol industry and the railroads. Women had long pushed for temperance laws, and the Prohibition amendment outlawing alcohol had been ratified in 1919. Meanwhile, the railroad industry worried that giving women the vote would result in stronger child labor laws and higher wages for women. Suffrage would have far-reaching implications across the country, and these business interests liked things just the way they were.

And so despite the new national law against the consumption of alcohol, many state representatives were taken to a private room on the eighth floor. It is unclear precisely what happened in that room, but many men left it utterly drunk and newly sympathetic to the anti-suffrage camp. Were they being bribed? No one knew for sure, but gradually every legislator the suffragists had identified as potentially vulnerable to bribes had switched sides. The opposition was fighting dirty.

Those who changed allegiances included the speaker of the Tennessee House, Seth Walker. Walker had long been a suffrage supporter, but now suddenly changed his mind. After hearing this news, a furious suffragist confronted him in the lobby of the Hermitage.

"What brought about your change?" she demanded. "The Louisville & Nashville Railroad?"

A red-faced Walker stormed out, but not before exclaiming, "That's an insult!"

Governor Roberts began the special session by urging passage of the amendment "in justice to the womanhood of America." After a few days of debates and committee meetings, the Senate was the first to vote. On Friday, August 13, it voted overwhelmingly in favor of ratification, 25–4. But while the US House of Representatives was suffrage friendly, opposition was strong in the Tennessee House. And the House wouldn't meet again until Monday.

So the battle stretched out over another weekend. Tension in the Hermitage, already at a fever pitch, ratcheted up another couple notches. The intense August heat meant most doors were kept open, and spies from both sides roamed the hallways.

After preliminary discussions, a final vote on ratification by the House was set for Wednesday, August 18. On August 17, the North Carolina legislature, as expected, voted down suffrage, which energized the "antis" in Tennessee. That night suffragists patrolled the Hermitage and even Nashville's train station to make sure none of their supporters got cold feet and suddenly snuck out of town. Anything was possible. Some legislators had even received fake messages asking them to come home. Rumors of kidnappings swirled. During the long night of the seventeenth, a number of activists gathered in Catt's room for one last strategy session. But the seasoned operative, with more than thirty years of organizing and activism to her name, had no more tricks up her sleeve. "There is one more thing we can do—only one," she said. "We can pray."

Expectant crowds had already gathered when the Tennessee House of Representatives came to session on August 18 at nine thirty in the morning. Suffragists' spirits were buoyed by the recent arrival from California of one pro-suffrage member of the Tennessee House. And another left his hospital bed to attend. All but three of the ninety-nine members of the House were in attendance. The suffragists had forty-seven "yes" votes they could count on—two short of ratification.

Barring a miracle, the suffragists were certain they would lose a very close vote.

After debate, Speaker Walker, who now opposed the amendment, rose, struck the gavel, and said, "The hour has come!" But then he called for a vote to table, or postpone, the bill, with hopes of preventing a vote on ratification itself.

Legislators were called in alphabetical order and voted by voice. Soon it appeared that the vote would be tabled and suffrage would lose. But when the vote got to Banks P. Turner, supposedly an "anti" legislator, he hesitated. Turner had been lobbied by both Governor Roberts and the Ohio governor earlier that morning. Rising slowly, he said, "I wish to be recorded as against the motion to table."

The vote ended in a 48–48 tie. The motion to table had failed. Suffrage was still alive. And Turner now supported ratification as well.

The actual vote to ratify the Nineteenth Amendment then began. Two ayes—votes for ratification—were quickly followed by four nays.

The seventh man called was Harry Burn. Only twenty-four years old, Burn was the youngest member of the House. He hailed from Mouse Creek, an eastern farm town hardly known for its support of suffrage. Burn was wearing a red rose, as were many other lawmakers—the War of the Roses had continued even inside the legislative chamber. Everyone expected Burn to vote against the amendment.

He responded to his name with a barely audible "Aye."

Had Burn gotten mixed up and said the wrong word?

No, he had not. What no one but Burn knew at the time was that he carried a letter from his mother in his pocket. He had received it that morning. Febb Ensminger Burn had never identified herself publicly as a suffrage supporter, but it turned out she had very firm opinions on the matter and she shared them with her son. Her short note read:

> *Hurrah, and vote for suffrage! Don't keep them in doubt. I notice some of the speeches against. They were bitter. I have been watching to see how you stood, but have not noticed anything yet. Don't forget to be a good boy. . . . Your Mother.*

Voting continued, and the suffragists soon realized that Burn's aye would make the difference. And indeed, the vote passed by the narrowest of margins: 49–47. The chamber erupted in pandemonium, the cheering and clapping so loud that Carrie Chapman Catt, who was waiting nervously back at the hotel, knew the results before the official messenger arrived. Tennessee was the thirty-sixth state to ratify the Nineteenth Amendment.

The battle was finally over. The vote had been won.

KNOW YOUR RADICALS:
∽ EDITH WILSON ∾

By the final year of his presidency, Woodrow Wilson was as obsessed with his goal as Alice Paul was with hers. But what was his goal exactly? After steering the country through the horrors of World War I and essentially saving Europe from itself, Wilson concluded that a new organization was required to prevent future wars of this sort. It would be called the "League of Nations," and its function would be to resolve international disputes before they led to violent conflict.

In the fall of 1919, Wilson traveled throughout the United States to drum up support for the treaty that would officially end World War I, a treaty that included forming the League of Nations. The plan was for him to travel eight thousand miles by rail in just twenty-two days, but the physical demands were too much for him. The president suffered headaches and eventually collapsed from exhaustion at a stop in Colorado in late September. Wilson made it back to Washington only to have a massive stroke on October 2. The stroke paralyzed the left side of his body and badly limited his vision.

The first official White House photo of President Wilson after his stroke with his wife, Edith, June 1920.

Edith Wilson, the president's second wife, found him on their bathroom floor the day of his stroke and immediately took control of the situation. In fact, she took control of much more than that. For the next year and a half, by keeping the full extent of his condition a secret from the press and almost everyone in government, Edith more or less ran the presidency. She decided which matters actually required the attention of the now-disabled president and took care of the rest herself.

Over time suspicions grew that something was wrong with the president. Wilson's Republican opponents did not approve of the new setup as they came to understand it. And at least one senator noted the irony of Woodrow Wilson, who had battled with suffrage activists for so long, being replaced by a woman: "The Presidentress . . . fulfilled the dream of the suffragettes by changing her title from First Lady to Acting First Man."

———⊛———

Early on the morning of August 26, 1920, and without ceremony, Secretary of State Bainbridge Colby signed the proclamation that certified the Nineteenth Amendment, at his home. All the years of work, all the sacrifice, all the frustration added just a single sentence to the US Constitution: "The right of citizens of the United States to vote shall not be denied or abridged by the United States or by any State on account of sex."

Throughout the process of state ratification, Alice Paul had been steadily sewing stars onto a flag, one for each state that voted yes. She had even allowed herself to be photographed in the process, though she normally avoided the limelight. The image of Paul seated and sewing like a traditional, domestic woman was a far cry from her reputation as the defiant head of the "militant" NWP. But Paul understood the American history she was a part of and chose in those final months to pay tribute to a great American woman, Betsy Ross, who is best known for having helped create the first American flag.

A short while after Colby made it official, Paul stepped out onto the balcony of her headquarters and presented her long, colorful flag, now complete with thirty-six stars.

Three months later she, along with millions of other American women, voted for the very first time in the presidential election.

Seventy-two years had passed since the signing of the Declaration of Sentiments in Seneca Falls. Charlotte Woodward, who was nineteen years old back in 1848 and was now ninety-one, was the only signer of that document alive to see the historic day when American women were given the legal right to vote. Sadly, she was too ill to vote on Election Day and would die before getting another chance. Like Lucretia Mott, Lucy

Alice Paul unfurls the suffrage flag she sewed at her headquarters in Washington, D.C., August 18, 1920.

Stone, Elizabeth Cady Stanton, and Susan B. Anthony, Woodward had fought for a right she herself never had the opportunity to exercise—though Carrie Chapman Catt, Lucy Burns, and Alice Paul did—as would so many generations of women to come, many of whom may not know a single one of these radicals' names.

But you do.

Epilogue

When the Nineteenth Amendment finally passed in 1920, Alice Paul was only thirty-five years old and would live another fifty-seven years, to the age of ninety-two. So what did she do for the last half century of her life?

Paul believed the Nineteenth Amendment was a great achievement, but that it could not change centuries of bias and discrimination toward women. She looked at the cluster of amendments that had been passed to ensure the rights of African Americans after the Civil War—the Thirteenth, Fourteenth, and Fifteenth—and concluded that women needed something similar. The only right guaranteed to women in the US Constitution is the right to vote.

In July 1923, which marked the seventy-fifth anniversary of the Seneca Falls Convention, the leaders of the National Woman's Party, including Paul, called a convention to discuss discrimination against women. At the convention, Paul proposed an amendment—then known as the "Lucretia Mott Amendment"—to the Constitution:

Men and women shall have equal rights throughout the United States and every place subject to its jurisdiction. Congress shall have power to enforce this article by appropriate legislation.

Paul understood that without a constitutional amendment guaranteeing equal rights, women were largely unable to defend themselves against discrimination in federal courts. Until the Equal Rights Amendment (ERA), as it came to be known, passed, women would not be equal to men. Paul spent the rest of her life fighting for its approval.

As with the Nineteenth Amendment, many women opposed the ERA. Some reformers felt this amendment would hurt the hard-fought gain women had made in laws protecting women and children in the workplace. Other women felt the ERA would destroy their ability to be supported by their husbands or mean that women could be drafted or sent into combat.

Nonetheless, in the early 1940s, the Republican and Democratic parties added the Equal Rights Amendment to their party platforms, in a show of political support for the idea that *"Equality of rights under the law shall not be denied or abridged by the United States or by any state on account of sex."* By 1943, the bill had become known as the Alice Paul Amendment.

In the 1960s a new women's rights movement took shape. Women began demanding equality under the law and the ERA gained more and more support. Finally, on March 22, 1972, forty-nine years after the Equal Rights Amendment was first introduced in Congress, it passed in the US House and the Senate. The proposed Twenty-Seventh Amendment to the Constitution now had to be ratified and that had to happen within the seven-year ratification deadline. Thirty-eight states had to ratify the amendment by 1979.

Twenty-two states ratified the ERA within a year. But after that the process slowed. Paul died in 1977, the same year Indiana became the thirty-fifth, and final, state to ratify the ERA. When the seven-year deadline arrived, the ERA was three states short.

Due to public pressure, Congress extended the deadline another three years to June 30, 1982. Meanwhile, in 1980, Republicans removed the Equal Rights Amendment from their platform; the party no longer supported ratification. Conservative political, religious, and business groups fought against passage of the bill. Unfortunately, no other state signed on during the extension period, despite protests, marches, civil disobedience, and hunger strikes.

However, supporters of the ERA have never stopped working. In 2017, Nevada ratified the ERA; Illinois followed in 2018. As of this writing, thirty-seven states have ratified the Equal Rights Amendment, one short of the thirty-eight needed for passage.

In early 2019, ERA supporters pinned their hopes on Virginia, whose state government was considering the bill. A December 2018 poll showed that 81 percent of Virginia's voters supported passage of the ERA. The bill passed in the Virginia Senate, with all nineteen Democratic members and seven Republican Senators voting in its favor. Passage looked good in the House of Delegates, the other part of Virginia's governing General Assembly, but a 50–50 tie meant defeat for ratification, which needed to have a majority vote. For all intents, the ERA was dead in Virginia.

Like the suffrage battle, the continuing struggle to add the ERA to the US Constitution is long, hard, and needs dedicated foot soldiers to work on passage of the bill. Supporters of the amendment understand that lawsuits will challenge the validity of ratification of the ERA after the 1982 deadline. But they carry on with the fight. As they were in the 2018 congressional election, more and more women will be elected on both a national and local basis. This is the grassroots support of local and state officials that will ultimately end with successful ratification of the ERA.

And as Susan B. Anthony said, "Failure is impossible."

Source Notes

CHAPTER 1

"Being the wife of a delegate . . .": Elizabeth Cady Stanton, *Eighty Years & More: Reminiscences 1815–1897* (New York: Schocken Books, 1971), 75.

"ladylike . . . Henry,": ibid., 74.

"pale and immovable . . . Oh my daughter . . .": Vivian Gornick, *The Solitude of Self: Thinking About Elizabeth Cady Stanton* (New York: Farrar, Straus and Giroux, 2006), 20.

"All that day and far into the night . . .": ibid.

"Everything we like to do is a sin . . .": Stanton, *Eighty Years & More*, 10.

"talk to the legislators . . .": ibid., 32.

"It is the custom . . . not to admit colored men . . .": Judith Wellman, *The Road to Seneca Falls: Elizabeth Cady Stanton and the First Woman's Rights Convention* (Urbana and Chicago: University of Illinois Press, 2004), 59–60.

"humiliated and chagrined,": Stanton, *Eighty Years & More*, 80.

"It was really pitiful . . .": ibid., 81.

"With all the thinking . . .": Gornick, *The Solitude of Self*, 26.

"In the eyes of the world . . .": ibid.

"the most important question . . .": Wellman, *The Road to Seneca Falls*, 48.

"unleashed her; thereafter . . .": ibid., 61.

"kept up a brisk fire morning . . .": ibid., 60.

"Calmly and skillfully Mrs. Mott . . .": ibid., 61.

"I sought every opportunity . . .": Geoffrey C. Ward and Ken Burns, *Not for Ourselves Alone: The Story of Elizabeth Cady Stanton and Susan B. Anthony* (New York: Alfred A. Knopf, 1999), 30.

"I love her now as belonging to us . . .": Lori D. Ginzberg, *Elizabeth Cady Stanton: An American Life* (New York: Hill and Wang, 2009), 39.

"The tantalizing tone . . . I shall never forget the look . . .": Wellman, *The Road to Seneca Falls*, 61.

"It was intensely gratifying . . .": Stanton, *Eighty Years & More*, 83.

"the movement for woman's suffrage . . .": Wellman, *The Road to Seneca Falls*, 63.

"as soon as we returned home . . .": Stanton, *Eighty Years & More*, 83.

KNOW YOUR RADICALS: ANNE HUTCHINSON

"a thing not tolerable . . . instrument of Satan . . . more bold than man,": Giles B. Gunn, ed., *Early American Writing* (New York: Penguin Classics, 1994), 159.

"You have no power over my body . . .": Eve LaPlante, *American Jezebel: The Life of Anne Hutchinson, the Woman Who Defied the Puritans* (New York: HarperOne, 2005), 120–21.

KNOW YOUR RADICALS: ABIGAIL ADAMS

"I long to hear that you have declared an independency . . .": John R. Vile, *Founding Documents of America: Documents Decode* (Santa Barbara, Calif.: ABC-CLIO, 2015), 89.

KNOW YOUR RADICALS: MARY WOLLSTONECRAFT

"Freedom, even uncertain freedom, is dear . . . You know I am not born to tread the beaten track.": George Robert Stirling Taylor, *Mary Wollstonecraft: A Study in Economics and Romance* (New York: Haskell House Publishers, 1969), 77.

CHAPTER 2

"How rapidly one throws off . . .": Stanton, *Eighty Years & More*, 143.

"male marriage,": Jean H. Baker, *Sisters: The Lives of America's Suffragists* (New York: Hill and Wang, 2005), 105.

"Motherhood is the most important . . .": Stanton, *Eighty Years & More*, 112.

"The real struggle was upon me...": ibid., 147.

"poured out...long-accumulating discontent... vehemence and indignation,": ibid., 148.

"stirred myself...as well as the rest of the party...": ibid.

"Why don't you do something about it?": Wellman, *The Road to Seneca Falls*, 189.

"public meeting for protest and discussion,": ibid.

"with much spirit and emphasis,": ibid., 192.

"The history of mankind is a history...": Mari Jo and Paul Buhle, eds., *The Concise History of Woman Suffrage* (Urbana and Chicago: University of Illinois Press, 1978), 94.

"we were rejoiced to find...": Wellman, *The Road to Seneca Falls*, 192.

"Resolved, that it is the duty...": Sally G. McMillen, *Seneca Falls and the Origins of the Women's Rights Movement* (New York: Oxford University Press, 2008), 240.

"thunderstruck...amazed at her daring...You will turn the proceedings into a farce...I must declare the truth as I believe it to be,": Wellman, *The Road to Seneca Falls*, 193.

"Why Lizzie...": McMillen, *Seneca Falls*, 93.

"Once the idea of suffrage had occurred...": Gornick, *The Solitude of Self*, 42.

"Depend upon it...this is the point to attack,": ibid.

"At first we travelled quite alone...": Miriam Gurko, *The Ladies of Seneca Falls: The Birth of the Woman's Rights Movement* (New York: Schocken Books, 1974), 99.

"right and duty...understand the height...": McMillen, *Seneca Falls*, 90.

"one of the most eloquent...": ibid., 92.

"more rational,": Buhle, eds., *The Concise History*, 97.

"The power to choose rulers...the right by which...": ibid.

"brilliant defense...he did not speak...": Wellman, *The Road to Seneca Falls*, 203.

"From 1848 on, Americans would be confronted...": ibid., 208.

PUTTING IT IN PERSPECTIVE: ABOLITIONISM

"I am a believer in that portion of the Declaration...": Jolyon P. Girard, Darryl Mace, and Courtney Smith, eds., *American History Through Its Greatest Speeches: A Documentary History of the United States* (Santa Barbara, Calif.: ABC-CLIO, 2016), 126.

KNOW YOUR RADICALS: THE GRIMKÉ SISTERS

"I must confess my womanhood...We are placed very unexpectedly...": Gurko, *The Ladies of Seneca Falls*, 40.

CHAPTER 3

"misconception, misrepresentation, and ridicule,": McMillen, *Seneca Falls*, 104.

"the most shocking and unnatural incident...": Elizabeth Frost and Kathryn Cullen-DuPont, *Women's Suffrage in America* (New York: Facts on File, 1992), 81.

"a most insane and ludicrous farce,": Penny Colman, *Elizabeth Cady Stanton and Susan B. Anthony: A Friendship That Changed the World* (New York: Square Fish, 2016), 48.

"A woman is nobody...": McMillen, *Seneca Falls*, 99.

"brilliant talents and excellent dispositions,": ibid., 98.

"There she stood...": Ginzberg, *Elizabeth Cady Stanton*, 78.

"I forged the thunderbolts...": Stanton, *Eighty Years & More*, 165.

"You stir up Susan...": McMillen, *Seneca Falls*, 109.

"big brain...In thought and sympathy...": Baker, *Sisters*, 87.

"single blessedness,": ibid., 65.

"I would not object to marriage...": ibid., 61.

"In her fifty-six years...": ibid., 76.

"With such women consecrating their lives...": ibid., 92.

"The nation's whole heart...": McMillen, *Seneca Falls*, 149.

"the first and only organization...": ibid., 155.

"If all that has been said by orators . . .": Carl Sandburg, *Abraham Lincoln: The Prairie Years and the War Years* (New York: Mariner Books, 2002), 484.

PUTTING IT IN PERSPECTIVE: BLOOMERS

"The attention of my audience . . .": Lynn Sherr, *Failure Is Impossible: Susan B. Anthony in Her Own Words* (New York: Times Books, 1996), 195.

CHAPTER 4

"We must take up . . .": Ginzberg, *Elizabeth Cady Stanton*, 119.

"The struggle of the last . . .": Gornick, *The Solitude of Self*, 80.

"May I ask just one question . . .": Ginzberg, *Elizabeth Cady Stanton*, 119.

"Buried in the citizen," ibid, 121.

"an outrage against women,": Baker, *Sisters*, 71.

"As the celestial gate . . . stand aside and see . . .": Ginzberg, *Elizabeth Cady Stanton*, 121–22.

"Their emancipation is . . . it is better to be . . . No; I would not trust him . . .": ibid., 122.

"My right as a human being . . .": Ann D. Gordon, ed., *The Selected Papers of Elizabeth Cady Stanton and Susan B. Anthony: Volume II, Against an Aristocracy of Sex, 1866 to 1873* (New Brunswick, N.J.: Rutgers University Press, 2000), 76.

"occupied a space . . .": McMillen, *Seneca Falls*, 168.

"accept aid even,": Gornick, *The Solitude of Self*, 86.

"aristocracy of sex,": Ginzberg, *Elizabeth Cady Stanton*, 127.

"The lower orders of men . . .": Buhle, eds., *The Concise History*, 254–55.

KNOW YOUR RADICALS: SOJOURNER TRUTH

"That man over there . . .": Eleanor Clift, *Founding Sisters and the Nineteenth Amendment* (Hoboken, N.J.: John Wiley & Sons, 2003), 25.

"I left everything behind . . .": Shirley Wilson Logan, ed., *With Pen and Voice: A Critical Anthology of Nineteenth-Century African-American Women* (Carbondale, Ill.: Southern Illinois University Press, 1995), 17.

"Look at me! Look at my arm! . . .": William Safire, ed., *Lend Me Your Ears: Great Speeches in History* (New York: W.W. Norton & Company, 2004), 685.

"I have borne thirteen children . . .":Logan, ed. *With Pen and Voice*, 24.

KNOW YOUR RADICALS: LUCY STONE

"A wife should no more . . .": Clift, *Founding Sisters*, 35.

"I wish, as a husband . . .": Alice Stone Blackwell, *Lucy Stone: Pioneer of Women's Rights* (Charlottesville, Va.: University of Virginia Press, 2007), 161.

"In behalf of the great principle . . .": ibid., 170.

CHAPTER 5

"Well I have been & gone . . . .": Sherr, *Failure Is Impossible*, 110.

"Without having a lawful right . . ." Ward and Burns, *Not for Ourselves Alone*, 142.

"Is this your usual method . . .": ibid.

"Oh, dear, no . . .": Clift, *Founding Sisters*, 54.

"I am traveling . . . Ask him for my fare,": ibid.

"Yes but I could . . .": ibid., 55.

"Has the prisoner anything . . .": Sherr, *Failure Is Impossible*, 115.

"Yes, your honor . . .": Ward and Burns, *Not for Ourselves Alone*, 145.

"The Court cannot allow . . .": ibid.

"political sovereigns,": Sherr, *Failure Is Impossible*, 116.

"The sentence of the Court . . .": ibid., 117.

"I shall never pay . . .": ibid.

"No matter how much women . . .": Gornick, *The Solitude of Self*, 7.

"an inferior being, subject to man,": Ward and Burns, *Not for Ourselves Alone*, 199.

"the complete emancipation of women,": McMillen, *Seneca Falls*, 233.

"How lonesome do I feel,": Ginzberg, *Elizabeth Cady Stanton*, 187.

KNOW YOUR RADICALS: VICTORIA WOODHULL

"If Congress refuse to listen . . .": Miriam Brody, *Victoria Woodhull: Free Spirit for Women's Rights* (New York: Oxford University Press, 2004), 70.

"scruffy white-trash relatives,": McMillen, *Seneca Falls*, 191.

CHAPTER 6

"completely shouted [Christabel] down . . . sang, yelled, whistled . . .": J. D. Zahniser and Amelia R. Fry, *Alice Paul: Claiming Power* (New York: Oxford University Press, 2014), 46.

"There is no Alice Paul . . .": Christine A. Lunardini, *From Equal Suffrage to Equal Rights: Alice Paul and the National Woman's Party, 1910–1928* (Lincoln, Neb.: iUniverse, 2000), 9.

"I remember hesitating the longest time . . .": Zahniser and Fry, *Alice Paul*, 1.

"The suffragettes threw themselves . . .": ibid., 70.

"Paul was the militant . . .": Clift, *Founding Sisters*, 97.

"one mind and spirit,": Lunardini, *From Equal Suffrage*, 16.

"One of the doctors stood . . .": Zahniser and Fry, *Alice Paul*, 99.

"master of spectacle,": Doris Stevens, *Jailed for Freedom: American Women Win the Vote* (Troutdale, Ore.: NewSage Press, 1995), 18.

"Where are the people? . . . Oh, they are out watching . . .": Baker, *Sisters*, 184.

"to march steadily . . .": ibid.

"We Demand an Amendment . . .": ibid.

"Dignity was about . . .": Zahniser and Fry, *Alice Paul*, 148.

"those ideals toward which both men and women . . .": Christine Lunardini, *Alice Paul: Equality for Women* (Boulder, Colo.: Westview Press, 2012), 55.

"one of the most impressively beautiful . . .": Clift, *Founding Sisters*, 92.

KNOW YOUR RADICALS: IDA B. WELLS

"As much as white women . . .": Marjorie Spruill Wheeler, ed., *One Woman, One Vote: Rediscovering the Woman Suffrage Movement* (Troutdale, Ore.: NewSage Press, 1995), 142.

CHAPTER 7

"the paramount . . . issue of the day,": Zahniser and Fry, *Alice Paul*, 164.

"But Mr. President . . .": ibid.

"This subject will receive . . .": Stevens, *Jailed for Freedom*, 37.

"the National Association will . . .": Zahniser and Fry, *Alice Paul*, 162.

"Not because we do not like . . .": ibid., 206.

"militant . . . un-American,": ibid., 187.

"what his position might . . .": Baker, *Sisters*, 205.

"I am not at liberty until I speak . . .": Zahniser and Fry, *Alice Paul*, 177.

"suffrage ought to be brought . . .": Stevens, *Jailed for Freedom*, 46.

"He kept us out of war . . . He kept us out of suffrage,": Baker, *Sisters*, 212.

"erratic heart,": Zahniser and Fry, *Alice Paul*, 251.

"It is impossible for me . . .": Clift, *Founding Sisters*, 122.

"We have got to take . . . We have got to bring . . .": Zahniser and Fry, *Alice Paul*, 255.

"Let us stand . . .": ibid.

"Mr. President, What Will . . . How Long Must . . .": Bernadette Cahill, *Alice Paul, the National Woman's Party, and the Vote: The First Civil Rights Struggle of the 20th Century* (Jefferson, N.C.: McFarland, 2015), 26.

"It will always be difficult . . .": Zahniser and Fry, *Alice Paul*, 263.

"Democracy must begin at Home . . .": ibid., 264.

"President Wilson and Envoy Root . . .": Baker, *Sisters*, 216.

"We have picketed . . . Has the law . . .": Stevens, *Jailed for Freedom*, 75.

"Not a dollar of your fine . . .": Clift, *Founding Sisters*, 131.

"We know full well . . .": Stevens, *Jailed for Freedom*, 80.

"Now that you women . . .": ibid., 86.

"Kaiser Wilson . . .": ibid., 88.

"The time has come . . .": Zahniser and Fry, *Alice Paul*, 280.

"I believe I never in my life . . .": Stevens, *Jailed for Freedom*, 118.

"Nothing short of the passage . . .": Lunardini, *From Equal Suffrage*, 137.

"We are put out of jail . . .": Zahniser and Fry, *Alice Paul*, 295.

CHAPTER 8

"The President had not felt...": Mary Walton, *A Woman's Crusade: Alice Paul and the Battle for the Ballot* (New York: St. Martin's Griffin, 2015), 209.

"Eleven to win...": Zahniser and Fry, *Alice Paul*, 302.

"Whenever we picketed...": Clift, *Founding Sisters*, 162.

"heartily in sympathy,": Katherine H. Adams and Michael L. Keene, *Alice Paul and the American Suffrage Campaign* (Urbana and Chicago: University of Illinois Press, 2008), 224.

"the burning indignation...": Zahniser and Fry, *Alice Paul*, 307.

"I shall do all that I can,": ibid.

"It is my duty...": Walton, *A Woman's Crusade*, 224.

"There was no excitement...": Clift, *Founding Sisters*, 179–80.

"Ratification in Tennessee...": Wheeler, *One Woman, One Vote*, 339.

"War of the Roses,": Clift, *Founding Sisters*, 193.

"What brought about... The Louisville... That's an insult!": Carol Lynn Yellin and Janaan Sherman, *The Perfect 36: Tennessee Delivers Woman Suffrage* (Oak Ridge, Tenn.: Iris Press, 1998), 97.

"in justice to the womanhood...": ibid., 98.

"There is one more thing... We can pray,": Wheeler, *One Woman, One Vote*, 346.

"The hour has come!": ibid.

"I wish to be recorded...": Yellin and Sherman, *The Perfect 36*, 106.

"Aye,": ibid., 117.

KNOW YOUR RADICALS: EDITH WILSON

"Hurrah, and vote...": Clift, *Founding Sisters*, 199.

"The Presidentress...": Nancy Hendricks, *America's First Ladies: A Historical Encyclopedia and Primary Document Collection of the Remarkable Women of the White House* (Santa Barbara, CA: ABC-CLIO, 2015), 234.

EPILOGUE

"Men and women shall have equal rights...": Cahill, *Alice Paul*, 119.

Bibliography

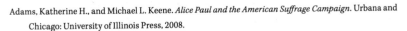

Adams, Katherine H., and Michael L. Keene. *Alice Paul and the American Suffrage Campaign*. Urbana and Chicago: University of Illinois Press, 2008.

Baker, Jean H. *Sisters: The Lives of America's Suffragists*. New York: Hill and Wang, 2005.

Blackwell, Alice Stone. *Lucy Stone: Pioneer of Women's Rights*. Charlottesville, Va.: University of Virginia Press, 2007.

Brody, Miriam. *Victoria Woodhull: Free Spirit for Women's Rights*. New York: Oxford University Press, 2004.

Buhle, Mari Jo, and Paul Buhle, eds. *The Concise History of Woman Suffrage*. Urbana and Chicago: University of Illinois Press, 1978.

Cahill, Bernadette. *Alice Paul, the National Woman's Party, and the Vote: The First Civil Rights Struggle of the 20th Century*. Jefferson, N.C.: McFarland, 2015.

Clift, Eleanor. *Founding Sisters and the Nineteenth Amendment*. Hoboken, N.J.: John Wiley & Sons, 2003.

Colman, Penny. *Elizabeth Cady Stanton and Susan B. Anthony: A Friendship That Changed the World*. New York: Square Fish, 2016.

Frost, Elizabeth, and Kathryn Cullen-DuPont. *Women's Suffrage in America*. New York: Facts on File, 1992.

Ginzberg, Lori D. *Elizabeth Cady Stanton: An American Life.* New York: Hill and Wang, 2009.

Girard, Jolyon P., Darryl Mace, and Courtney Smith, eds. *American History Through Its Greatest Speeches: A Documentary History of the United States.* Santa Barbara, Calif.: ABC-CLIO, 2016.

Gordon, Ann D., ed. *The Selected Papers of Elizabeth Cady Stanton and Susan B. Anthony: Volume II, Against an Aristocracy of Sex, 1866 to 1873.* New Brunswick, N.J.: Rutgers University Press, 2000.

Gornick, Vivian. *The Solitude of Self: Thinking About Elizabeth Cady Stanton.* New York: Farrar, Straus and Giroux, 2006.

Gunn, Giles B., ed. *Early American Writing.* New York: Penguin Classics, 1994.

Gurko, Miriam. *The Ladies of Seneca Falls: The Birth of the Woman's Rights Movement.* New York: Schocken Books, 1974.

Hendricks, Nancy. *America's First Ladies: A Historical Encyclopedia and Primary Document Collection of the Remarkable Women of the White House.* Santa Barbara, Calif.: ABC-CLIO, 2015.

LaPlante, Eve. *American Jezebel: The Life of Anne Hutchinson, the Woman Who Defied the Puritans.* New York: HarperOne, 2005.

Logan, Shirley Wilson, ed. *With Pen and Voice: A Critical Anthology of Nineteenth-Century African American Women.* Carbondale, Ill.: Southern Illinois University Press, 1995.

Lunardini, Christine. *Alice Paul: Equality for Women.* Boulder, Colo.: Westview Press, 2012

Lunardini, Christine A. *From Equal Suffrage to Equal Rights: Alice Paul and the National Woman's Party, 1910–1928.* Lincoln, Neb.: iUniverse, 2000.

McMillen, Sally G. *Seneca Falls and the Origins of the Women's Rights Movement.* New York: Oxford University Press, 2008.

Safire, William, ed. *Lend Me Your Ears: Great Speeches in History.* New York: W.W. Norton & Company, 2004.

Sandburg, Carl. *Abraham Lincoln: The Prairie Years and the War Years.* New York: Mariner Books, 2002.

Sherr, Lynn. *Failure Is Impossible: Susan B. Anthony in Her Own Words.* New York: Times Books, 1996.

Stanton, Elizabeth Cady. *Eighty Years & More: Reminiscences 1815–1897.* New York: Schocken Books, 1971.

Stevens, Doris. *Jailed for Freedom: American Women Win the Vote.* Troutdale, Ore.: NewSage Press, 1995.

Taylor, George Robert Stirling. *Mary Wollstonecraft: A Study in Economics and Romance.* New York: Haskell House Publishers, 1969.

Vile, John R. *Founding Documents of America: Documents Decode.* Santa Barbara, Calif.: ABC-CLIO, 2015.

Walton, Mary. *A Woman's Crusade: Alice Paul and the Battle for the Ballot.* New York: St. Martin's Griffin, 2015.

Ward, Geoffrey C., and Ken Burns. *Not for Ourselves Alone: The Story of Elizabeth Cady Stanton and Susan B. Anthony.* New York: Alfred A. Knopf, 1999.

Wellman, Judith. *The Road to Seneca Falls: Elizabeth Cady Stanton and the First Woman's Rights Convention.* Urbana and Chicago: University of Illinois Press, 2004.

Wheeler, Marjorie Spruill, ed. *One Woman, One Vote: Rediscovering the Woman Suffrage Movement.* Troutdale, Ore.: NewSage Press, 1995.

Yellin, Carol Lynn, and Janaan Sherman. *The Perfect 36: Tennessee Delivers Woman Suffrage.* Oak Ridge, Tenn.: Iris Press, 1998.

Zahniser, J. D., and Amelia R. Fry. *Alice Paul: Claiming Power.* New York: Oxford University Press, 2014.

Three suffragists cast votes in New York City, circa 1917.

Acknowledgments

How special when your oldest childhood friend makes a dream come true for you. Amy Berkower, of Writers House, did just that. Ken Wright, VP and publisher of Viking Children's Books, put the dream into action. My husband, Steve Auerbach, helped research and make this book. Todd Hasak-Lowy worked magic shaping the words and story. Catherine Frank and Genevieve Gagne-Hawes made sure that story was pure. Alice Martin, of Writers House, Sheila Keenan, Nancy Brennan, Janet Pascal, Laura Steirs, and others behind the scenes at Viking, helped shape the project.

A big-hearted hug to Sally Roesch Wagner for being a part of this book. You are a source of inspiration. Thanks to Deborah Hughes, Marilyn Tedeschi, Esther Cohn, Maria Ellis, Terry Blosser-Bernardo, Marguerite Kearns, Trudy Mason, and Senator Betty Little.

My parents, Roz and Jack Zimet, made me the woman I am with their love and constant encouragement. Andrew, Hannah, Steve, Kim, and Grover, you are my life. Victor, Robert, Jake, and Ajed Zimet; Linda Auerbach; Stephanie Silber; Linda Hanway; Ian, Darlene, Emily, and Elyssa Malings, you are all a part of who I am and I love you all.

And to all my extended family and friends, you round out my life. Thank you for helping bring this important story to readers. Enjoy, get involved, and remember to vote!

Index

Page numbers in *italics* indicate photographs and illustrations.

abolitionism
    and Anthony, 47
    and Gage, 87
    and Grimké sisters, 39–41
    influence on women's movement, 34–35
    and origins of women's movement, 23, 26
    and postwar politics, 54, 55, 59
    and Quakerism, 17, 28, 34
    and Stone, 64
    and World Anti-Slavery Convention, 7–9
Adams, Abigail, *15*, 15–16
Adams, John, 15–16
African Americans, 13, 39, 58, 104, 106–8, 138, 147. *See also* racism and racial politics
amendment campaigns
    and Congressional Union activism, 115–17
    and court battles for suffrage, 79
    and Equal Rights Amendment, 147–48
    and leadership of the suffrage movement, 101
    and the National Woman's Rights Convention, 62–63
    and Paul's leadership, 92
    and picket campaigns, 121–23, 123–27
    and political pressure on Wilson, 133–36
    and radical suffrage activism, 104, 118–20
    and ratification of Nineteenth Amendment, 136–39, 139–43, 145–46
    and state suffrage efforts, 67–69
    successes in Congress, 89
    and tensions within suffrage movement, 114
    and votes on Nineteenth Amendment, 129–33
American Anti-Slavery Society, 34, 56–57, 64
American Equal Rights Association (AERA), 62, 67–68, 72
American Woman Suffrage Association (AWSA), 72, 73, 79–80
Anthony, Susan B., *48, 50*, 149, 150
    background, 47–48

    and bloomers, 45–46
    and court battles for suffrage, 73–79
    and Gage, 87
    influence on author's life, 4
    influence on younger suffragists, 88–90, 98, 116
    leadership of, 42, 53–54
    and leadership of suffrage movement, 101
    and origins of women's rights movement, 27
    and Paul's activism, 95
    and picket campaigns, 122
    and postwar politics, 54, 56–58
    and racism in suffrage movement, 63, 71, 72
    and radical suffrage activism, 103
    and the Rochester Convention, 46–49
    and the Seneca Falls Convention, 41
    Stanton contrasted with, 83–85
    Stanton's partnership with, 42, 49–52
    and state suffrage efforts, 67–69
    and Stone, 65, 66
    and votes on Nineteenth Amendment, 135, 146
    and the Women's Party, 117
    and Woodhull, 81, 82
Asquith, H. H., 97
Avery, Rachel Foster, 80

Baumfree, Isabella. *See* Truth, Sojourner
Beecher, Henry Ward, *82*
Blackwell, Alice Stone, 80
Blackwell, Elizabeth, 86–87
Blackwell, Henry, 65–68, 86–87
Blatch, Harriot Stanton, 119
Bloomer, Amelia, 37, 44–46
bloomers, 44–46, *45*
Blyth, Benjamin, *15*
Boston, Massachusetts, 23
Burn, Febb Ensminger, 143
Burn, Harry, 143
Burns, Lucy, *99*

and Congressional Union activism, 115–16

and Gage, 88

and leadership of suffrage movement, 100–102

and Paul's activism, 97–99

and picket campaigns, 122–23, 125–26

and radical suffrage activism, 103, 109, 111, 113–14

and ratification of Nineteenth Amendment, 146

Bush, Abigail, 44

—

Cady, Daniel, 9–10

Cady, Eleazer, 9–10

Catt, Carrie Chapman, *91*

and Anthony's influence, 88–89

and leadership of suffrage movement, 101

and NAWSA leadership, 113–15

and political compromise, 92

and ratification of Nineteenth Amendment,
      136–37, 138–39, 141, 143, 146

and votes on Nineteenth Amendment, 135

Church of England, 11, 27–28

Civil War, 35, 54–56, 58

Claflin, Tennessee, 80–81

Colby, Bainbridge, 145

Congressional Union (CU), 114–15

Cosu, Alice M., 126

Cotton, John, 11

—

Daughters of Temperance, 47

Day, Dorothy, 126

Declaration of Independence, 16, 26, 30–31, 34–35

Declaration of Sentiments, 31–32, 36–37, 41–43, 54, 146

Delta Sigma Theta, 105

Democratic Party, 68–69, 115, 117, 132–33, 138

De Priest, Oscar, 108

Dessier, William, *45*

Douglass, Frederick, *38*, 38–39, 43, 70, 82

Dukakis, Michael, 13

—

Equal Rights Amendment, 148–150

Equal Rights Party, 81–82

—

Fifteenth Amendment, 71, 72, 147

Fillmore, Millard, 77

Fourteenth Amendment

adoption of, 71

and court battles for suffrage, 73–74, 79, 81

and the Equal Rights Amendment campaign, 147

proposed, 62

and racism in the South, 138

"franchise" (term), 32–33, 52–53, 67

"free love," 81

Freemasons' Hall (London), 9, 13, 17, 18–19

French Revolution, 19–20, 25

Fugitive Slave Law, 87

—

Gage, Henry, 87

Gage, Matilda Joslyn, 86–87, *87*

Garrison, William Lloyd, 34, 47

Grimké, Angelina, 39–41, *40*, 48, 64

Grimké, Sarah, 39–41, *40*, 48, 64

—

Harper, Frances, 106

Harper, Ida Husted, 87

Heffelfinger, Kate, *126*

The Hermitage, 139–41

House Judiciary Committee, 81

Hughes, Charles Evans, 117

hunger strikes, 99–100, *124*, 124–25, 127

Hunt, Jane, 26, 28

Hunt, Richard, 26, 29

Hunt, Ward, 77

Hutchinson, Anne Marbury, 11–13, 48

Hutchinson, Susanna, 12–13

Hutchinson, William, 11

—

Independence Square, 134

"Is It a Crime for a Citizen of the United States to
      Vote?" (Anthony), 76–77

—

Jim Crow laws, 70

—

Lawrence, David, 127

League of Nations, 134, 144

Lewis, Dora, 126

The Lily, 45

Lincoln, Abraham, 35, 55–56, *61*

Lockwood, Belva, 83

Louis X, 34

"Lucretia Mott Amendment," 147

lynchings, 107–8

—

marriage

and Adams, 15–16

Anthony on, 50–51, 54

and Gage, 87

and legal status of women, 4

and property rights of women, 25–26
and social fears of suffrage, 138
and Stanton, 9, 10, 22–23, 49
and Stone, 65–67
and Truth, 59
and Woodhull, 81
Married Women's Property Act, 25–26
Massachusetts Bay Colony, 12
M'Clintock, Elizabeth, 26, 30, 44
M'Clintock, Mary Ann, 26
Milholland, Inez, 103, *104*, 118, *118*
Miller, Elizabeth Smith, 44, 45
Minor, Virginia, 79
Mott, James, 37
Mott, Lucretia, *17*
    and influence of abolitionist movement, 34
    and origins of women's rights movement, 21–23,
        26–27, 29–30
    and ratification of Nineteenth Amendment, 146
    and the Seneca Falls Convention, 33, 37, 41
    and sexism, 48
    Stanton's introduction to, 17–19

National American Woman Suffrage Association
    (NAWSA)
    and court battles for suffrage, 80
    and Gage, 88
    and leadership failings, 101
    and political compromise, 92
    and racism in suffrage movement, 70
    and radical suffrage activism, 109
    and ratification of Nineteenth Amendment, 136, 139
    and Stanton's writings, 85
    and state elections, 133
    successes in US Congress, 89
    and tensions within suffrage movement, 113–15
    and votes on Nineteenth Amendment, 135
    and World War I years, 121
National Equal Rights Party, 83
National Woman's Party (NWP)
    and the Equal Rights Amendment campaign, 147
    headquarters, *118*
    and picket campaigns, 123
    political activism of, 116–18, 121
    and ratification of Nineteenth Amendment, 139, 145
    and state elections, 133–34

National Woman's Rights Convention, 62
National Woman Suffrage Association (NWSA), 72,
    79–80, 81, 87–88
New York State Constitution, 67
Nineteenth Amendment ("Anthony Amendment")
    and activist strategies, 104, 116
    and electoral politics, 117
    and pressure on Wilson, 113
    ratification of, 136–39, 139–43, 145–46
    state-by-state strategy contrasted with, 92
    and varied suffrage strategies, 79, 101, 114
    votes on, 89, 115, 129–33, 134–36, 146
North Star, 38, 43

Occoquan Workhouse, 122, 124–27, *126*, 129

Pankhurst, Christabel, 93–100, 102, 105, 120
Pankhurst, Emmeline, 94–100, 102,, 120
Paul, Alice, *96*
    arrest and imprisonment, 126–27
    and Congressional Union activism, 115–16
    and the Equal Rights Amendment, 147–49
    and Gage, 88
    and leadership of suffrage movement, 100–102, 144
    Pankhursts' influence on, 95–100
    and picket campaigns, 121–22, 123–25
    political background, 93–95
    and political pressure on Wilson, 133–35
    and presidential elections, 117
    and radical suffrage activism, 92, 102–3, 103–4,
        108–9, 119–20
    and ratification of Nineteenth Amendment, 136,
        139, 145–46, *146*
    and state elections, 133
    and tensions within suffrage movement, 113–15
    and votes on Nineteenth Amendment, 130–32
    and Wilson's meeting with suffragists, 111–13
Pearson, Josephine Anderson, 139
Phillips, Wendell, 13–14, 57–59
picket campaigns, 119–25, *120*, 127, 131–32
prison sentences of activists
    and antislavery activism, 87
    and Burns, 98–100
    and court battles for suffrage, 77–78
    and hunger strikes, *124*
    and picket campaigns, 122, 124–28, *126*, 129, 132

property rights, 4–5, 10–12, 15, 25–26, 54

publicity and public opinion

    and anti-suffrage cartoons, *55*

    and bloomers, 45–46

    and court battles for suffrage, 78

    and origins of women's rights movement, 29–30

    and radical suffrage activism, 118–20

    and the Seneca Falls Convention, 38–39, 43

    and votes on Nineteenth Amendment, 132

    and Wells, 107–8

Puck, *55, 110*

Punch, 45–46

———

Quakerism

    and abolitionism, 17, 28, 34

    and Anthony, 46

    and Mott, 17

    and origins of women's rights movement, 27–28

    and Paul, 93

    and Truth, 59

———

racism and racial politics

    and the Civil War Amendments, 147

    and lynchings in the South, 107–8

    and postwar politics, 71–72

    and radical suffrage activism, 104–5

    and ratification of Nineteenth Amendment, 138

    and state suffrage efforts, 68–69

    and tensions within suffrage movement, 63–64,
        69–71

ratification of the 19th Amendment, 136–39, *137,*
    139–43, 145–46

reform movements, 27–28

religious beliefs

    and Gage, 88

    and Grimké sisters, 40–41

    and Hutchinson, 11–13

    and marriage customs, 9

    and Quakerism, 27–28

    and Stanton, 84–85

    and Truth, 60

    See also Quakerism

Republican Party, 68, 117, 145

The Revolution, 71

Roberts, Albert H., 139, 141, 142

Rochester, New York, 4, 43–44, 46

Roosevelt, Theodore, 85

Root, Elihu, 121

Ross, Betsy, 145–46

———

segregation, 70, 104–5

Seneca County Courier, 29–30

Seneca Falls, New York

    and impact of women's rights convention, 43–44

    and influence of Adams, 16

    key resolutions of, 30–33

    and origins of women's rights movement, 26,
        29–30, 32–33, 36–39, 41

    Stanton's move to, 24

sexism

    and the abolition movement, 8–9

    and Anthony's background, 48–49

    and domestic violence, 4–5

    and the Equal Rights Amendment, 147

    and postwar politics, 71–72

    sexual violence and harassment, 5

    and Stanton's background, 8–10

    and suffrage activism, 90–91

Shaw, Anna Howard, 101, 113–15

Shoup, Oliver Henry, *137*

Silent Sentinels, 120–23

slavery, 28, 54, 60, 61. *See also* abolitionism

"The Solitude of the Self" (Stanton), 84

Stanton, Daniel, *24,* 63

Stanton, Elizabeth Cady, *8, 24, 50*

    background, 9–10

    and bloomers, 44–46

    and complexity of suffrage battle, 90

    and court battles for suffrage, 73–74

    and domestic life, 25–26

    and Gage, 87–88

    and influence of abolitionist movement, 34

    influence on younger suffragists, 116

    and leadership of suffrage movement, 53, 101

    literary contributions, 83–85

    Mott's introduction to, 17–19

    and origins of women's rights movement, 21–29

    Pankhursts' influence on, 98

    partnership with Anthony, 42, 49–52

    and postwar politics, 54, 56–59, 71–72

    and racism in suffrage movement, 62–64

    and radical suffrage activism, 119

    and ratification of Nineteenth Amendment, 146

    and the Rochester Convention, 46–49

and the Seneca Falls Convention, 30–33, 36–39, 41

and state suffrage efforts, 68–69

and Stone, 66

and Woodhull's presidential bid, 82

and the World Anti-Slavery Convention, 7–9, 13–15

Stanton, Harriot, *8*

Stanton, Henry, 7–9, 22–24, 33, 50, 56

states' rights, 138

Stone, Lucy, *65*

　background, 64–67

　and bloomers, 45–46

　and Gage, 86–87

　and leadership of suffrage movement, 101

　and racism in suffrage movement, 71

　and ratification of Nineteenth Amendment, 146

　and state suffrage efforts, 67–68, 79

"suffrage" (term), 32–33, 52

——

temperance movement, 23, 35, 47–49, 54, 87, 140

Tennessee, 129, 137–39, 139–43

Tennessee State Association Opposed to Woman
　　Suffrage, 139

Terrell, Mary Church, 105, 106

Thirteenth Amendment, 55, 58, 62, 147

Tilton, Elizabeth, 82

Train, George Francis, 68–69

The Trial of Susan B. Anthony (Anthony), 79

trials of suffrage activists, 11–12, *12*, 73, 74–79, 87, 122

Truth, Sojourner, 59–62, *60, 61*

Turner, Banks P., 142

Twenty-Seventh Amendment (proposed), 148

——

Underground Railroad, 86, 87

United States v. Susan B. Anthony, 77–79

universal suffrage (term), 52–53, 62, 67, 70

US Congress, 43, 58, 111–12, 114–15, 134. *See also* US
　　House of Representatives; US Senate

US Constitution, 62, 79–80, 134, 145. *See also specific*
　　amendments

US House of Representatives

　and Congressional Union activism, 115

　and court battles for suffrage, 79–81

　and the Equal Rights Amendment, 148

　and postwar politics, 58

　and ratification of Nineteenth Amendment, 141

　and votes on Nineteenth Amendment, 129–31,
　　　134–36

US Senate

　and Congressional Union activism, 115

　and court battles for suffrage, 79–80

　and the Equal Rights Amendment, 148

　and equal suffrage, 52

　and postwar politics, 58

　and ratification of Nineteenth Amendment, 141

　and votes on Nineteenth Amendment, 131–36

US Supreme Court, 76–77, 79

——

A Vindication of the Rights of Men (Wollstonecraft), 20

A Vindication of the Rights of Woman (Wollstonecraft), 20

violence against women, 4–5, 106, 123–24

——

Walker, Seth, 140–42

"War of the Roses," 139, *140*, 143

Weld, Theodore Dwight, 40

Wells, Ida B., 104–5, 106–8

Whittaker, Raymond, 122–23, 125

Whole World Temperance Convention, 48

Williams, Roger, 12

Wilson, Edith, *144*, 144–45

Wilson, John, 11–12

Wilson, Woodrow, *144*

　meeting with suffragists, 111–13

　stroke, 144–45

　suffrage activism aimed at, 102, 103–4, 109, 115,
　　　117, 118–20, 121–23, 123–25, 127

　support for amendment efforts, 129, 131–33,
　　　133–35

Winthrop, John, 11–12, 13

Wollstonecraft, Mary, 19–20, 48

The Woman's Bible (Stanton), 84–85

Woman's Rights Convention, 54, 87

Women's Loyal National League (WLNL), 54–55

Women's National Liberal Union, 88

Women's Social and Political Union (WSPU), 94, 95, 101

Woodhull, Canning, 81

Woodhull, Victoria, 80–83, *82*

Woodward, Charlotte, 36, 41, 146

World Anti-Slavery Convention, 7–9, 13–15, 17–22,
　　57–58

World War I, 117, 121, 129

Wright, Martha, 26, 54

——

Younger, Maud, 136